Up a Creek, With a Paddle
Tales of Canoeing and Life

James W. Loewen

Up a Creek, With a Paddle: Tales of Canoeing and Life
James W. Loewen
© 2020 PM Press

ISBN: 978-1-62963-827-0 (print)
ISBN: 978-1-62963-843-0 (ebook)
Library of Congress Control Number: 2020934735

Cover by John Yates / www.stealworks.com
Interior design by briandesign

10 9 8 7 6 5 4 3 2 1

PM Press
PO Box 23912
Oakland, CA 94623
www.pmpress.org

Printed in the USA

The author thanks Annemie Curlin for her portrait of me on the next page and the drawing of the tree in "Paddling the Boundary Waters." Her brother Hans Bednar did all the other illustrations in the book, for which I am very grateful. They are brother and sister, still close although separated by an ocean. (Hans lives in Austria, Annemie in Vermont.) Annemie has been my close friend for 45 years and Hans for 45 days, and both have blessed my life.

I also would like to credit the following persons who let me tell stories including them, hopefully not to their permanent detriment: Wendell Brase, John Duell, David Shiman, Karen Edwards, Gail Wheeler, Trish Duell, and Susan Loewen. Also, two exemplary readers commented on the entire manuscript: Dick Atlee and Lucy L. McMurrer. Joey Paxman and Gregory Nipper at PM Press made the book happen, professionally and rapidly. Thanks to you all! Finally, I thank all those who organized the trips I've taken in Vermont and the DC metropolitan area, as well as the Potomac and Shenandoah Riverkeepers, who try mightily to save and even improve the Chesapeake watershed so it can be enjoyed.

The author at the peak of his paddling powers, such as they were.

Contents

Introduction

This little book offers a fine launch into the sport of canoeing, so long as the reader does not imitate *any* of the actions herein described. Read as a series of cautionary tales, it provides an introduction to river safety as well. Almost every chapter asks the rhetorical question, "What could possibly go wrong?" and then proceeds to find surprising answers.

Despite these misadventures, or maybe because of them, canoeing gave me more than half a century of fun, fellowship with others, and contact with nature. A river offers perhaps the closest analogy to life. It has periods of excitement and boredom, bad and even scary happenings, and good and even beautiful experiences. Like life, it flows only forward.

Like the annual cycles of seasons in life, a river is similar when paddled again, but never the same. As Heraclitus famously wrote, 2,500 years ago, "No man ever steps in the same river twice, for it's not the same river and he's not the same man." You can never undo a mistake on a river. You can only move on, possibly doing better next time. Perhaps that also holds for life.

Rapids are classified by how easy they are to negotiate, from Class I—no maneuvering required—to Class VI—passable only by world-class paddlers in decked kayaks. Canoeing a rapid, even a mild Class I, compels you to be present, to "be here now," as the hippies used to say (and maybe still do). Being present is one of the joys of existence, not just canoeing. Being present in nature is best of all.

A canoeing T-shirt I own makes an overt parallel between canoeing and life: "Life is short," it says. "Paddle hard."[1] Being present in society is also essential to living a fulfilled, meaningful life. Mere alienation will not do. Theodore Roosevelt may have been right when he wrote, "The greatest gift life has to offer is the opportunity to work hard at work worth doing."

I worked hard at work worth doing. Or at least I think I did, and I think it was. Owing to an unfortunate medical prognosis, this is the only memoir I'm likely to finish, so after some episodes I have added "reflections," in which my sociological ideas fight to the surface, triggered by the canoeing experience. A later part of the book will assess my work, not just my canoeing. I will include some comments from readers who claim that my work changed their lives. Maybe those of you who have liked my writings will take pleasure from learning some of the reactions of others. Maybe those of you who don't yet know my work will take pleasure from these canoeing tales and then try a more serious volume.

I do hope this book doesn't put you off canoeing. Rather, on some weekend when the weather is too unpleasant to venture out, I hope it gives you at least a few chuckles, if not a real laugh. Maybe it will also whet your appetite to construct some paddling memories of your own. I also hope you are creating some life stories of successful completion of tasks worth doing.

I ended *Lies My Teacher Told Me* with the phrase "Bon voyage to us both!" I shall not end this memoir with the same phrase, because my life nears its close. Instead, I would suggest to you the phrase that has become my email signoff: "There is a reciprocal relationship between truth about the past and justice in the present. Telling the truth about the past helps cause justice in the present. Achieving justice in the present helps us tell the truth about the past." Those sentences have helped me see strategic ways to work to change our society for the better. Maybe they'll be useful to you, too, as you journey on ahead of me. Maybe this little book will be a mild blessing, too, on *that* voyage. I hope so.

Notes

1   As the chapter "Paddle Hard" explains, actually it says, "Life's too short." I took poetic license.

A River So Narrow
We Paddled on Land

When I was young, I was a Boy Scout. I'm glad I was a Boy Scout. I learned lots about nature and camping, some of which I still remember.[1]

One of the best ways to experience both nature and camping is on a canoe trip. As a Boy Scout, I earned my canoeing merit badge. Then, after I turned fourteen and became an Explorer Scout, I went to Region Seven Canoe Base in northern Wisconsin, for a weeklong canoe trip. "Canoe Base," as we called it, was located on White Sand Lake, just south of Michigan's Upper Peninsula and just south of a very interesting continental divide.[2] White Sand Lake and its outlet, White Sand Creek, connect to the Manitowish River, which ultimately flows into the Mississippi River and ends in the Gulf of Mexico south of New Orleans. To the north, the Presque Isle River flows into Lake Superior, and all the Great Lakes wind up draining into the St. Lawrence River, ending in the Gulf of St. Lawrence near Newfoundland. Unlike most continental divides, the land is rather flat, mostly covered by lakes and marshes. A short portage can take paddlers from a lake that drains south to one draining north while leaving them unaware of the transition.

In an unpretentious way, the land is beautiful. In summer its varied shades of green are so vivid they seem they might damage the eyes. Some of the marshes include pitcher plants and sundews, plants famed for eating insects.

The rivers and lakes are so clear you can sometimes step out of a canoe into what you think is two feet of water, only to go in over your head. I loved it. Later, when I was old enough, I mailed in an application to work on the Canoe Base staff.

They hired me! I was excited, although my exact post turned out to be dishwasher, and my pay was the exact sum of $113, not for a week, nor even a month, but for the entire summer. (Yes, I know money was worth more then. Still . . .)

But I worked my way up, and by my fourth year I was in charge of the Service Department. The camp staff was divided into three departments: service, training, and trail. The Service Department was largest. We took care of the dining hall, dispensed the food for all meals on the trail, maintained the buildings and grounds, staffed the trading post (which made money selling souvenirs and snacks to canoe campers), and provided other camp functions. Explorer Scout groups went on one-week trips, and the trainers gave one camper from each group four days of training ahead of time, teaching everything from how to lash paddles in a canoe before portaging to how to start a fire in the rain. The Trail Department was in charge of the vehicles and providing put-ins and pick-ups for groups at the start and end of their weeklong trips.

One of the reasons I wanted to work at Canoe Base was so I could go canoeing. But since I worked in the Service Department, I could only go canoeing on my day off. And even then, the Trail Department, always looking for new routes for our campers, would only give us transportation if we were willing to go to places useful to them. This meant they put us in on creeks and portages Canoe Base was not already using—routes they wanted to check out for future trips.

Usually there proved to be good reasons why we were not already using them.

On one occasion, Ed, the head of the Trail Department, talked four of us into descending the East Branch of the Presque Isle River, in two canoes.[3] The Presque Isle ran parallel to an itinerary we were already using, a route requiring portaging from lake to lake. If we could use the river, that would give our groups a loop—a way to paddle 50 miles without requiring a long drive to put them in or pick them up. That would be very useful to the Trail Department.

Besides, what could possibly go wrong? It's a *river*, after all, not a mere creek, Ed pointed out.

He drove us to the put-in. Right away, we could see what might go wrong. The "river" was only four feet wide! Since canoes are only three feet wide, ours could fit in OK, but we couldn't fit our paddles in the river as well. Mostly we kind of poled against the sides of the "river" banks.

I expressed doubts. "There's almost no water," I said. "This might be a predicament in the making."

Ed brushed aside my complaints. "There's plenty of water," he replied. "Look how deep it is. Besides, we've come all the way out here," he noted. "We need to have something to show for it."

So we set off. For a while, we did OK, paddling and poling on the banks, as the stream wound its way through a picturesque flat meadow. Then we reached the edge of the woods, where we also reached the reason why we had plenty of water: the first beaver dam. We portaged over the dam. Fortunately, the stream widened out a bit below the dam. Unfortunately, it therefore became shallower, so we then had to walk our canoes downriver for maybe a hundred yards. Then the water stopped flowing as much and became deeper as we reached the backwater from the next beaver dam. We got in and paddled again.

We continued this way over two or three more beaver dams, each affording us maybe half a mile of paddling. To be fair to Ed, the creek had widened out some, so we didn't have to pole on the bank anymore. We ate lunch and had a good time.

Then we reached the grandfather of all beaver dams. Actually, we weren't sure it *was* a beaver dam. The creek simply disappeared into a tremendous deadfall. At the bottom were the smaller logs and branches surely placed by beavers. Then came entire trees, once 30 and 60 feet tall, that had crashed down in some heavy wind, we thought, or perhaps had been left by a legendary flood. There was no pulling our canoes over that layer, however, because still more downed trees crisscrossed the creek to at least fifteen feet above it! We would have had to be aerialists to lift our canoes over that barricade.[4] Only with a chainsaw could we have gotten through it. And there were even deadfalls in the woods! So there was no way to portage around this obstacle, either.

We reconnoitered. To our right we knew there was a Forest Service road. Eventually a car might drive down it and give us a ride to some place—a town, a resort, or at least a private home—with a phone. Remember, this was decades before cell phones, which often don't work in wilderness areas anyway.

With difficulty, we portaged our canoes through the woods and around the deadfalls to the road. Then we were supposed to walk west to a cluster of houses down a little road on a lake—Ed had told us that these were sure to have a phone. I volunteered for this task, walking off a couple of miles to the west. I crossed a road coming from the south but continued dutifully toward the houses.

Later, unknown to me, a car drove up that road, turned east, and came upon our canoes and the other three paddlers. It picked up two of them, leaving one person with the canoes, and took them eventually to a phone; they called Canoe Base.

Meanwhile, I reached the cutoff for the cluster of houses but noticed no utility line going in—this was a group of rustic cabins with no electricity, no phone. Twilight was approaching. What to do?

While I pondered, a car came along this almost-deserted forestry road, and the driver gave me a ride to Marenisco, a tiny town in Michigan just north of the Wisconsin state line. By the time I arrived, the only establishment still open was an all-night laundromat, with one customer, but luckily it had a pay phone. I called Canoe Base and reached Ed, who was not happy with me. Eventually someone from the Trail Department picked me up; of course, they had already picked up the canoes and my three fellow paddlers. It was nearing midnight when I got back to the base.

The next morning I went in to talk with Ed. "Did you have a problem with me yesterday?" I asked.

"I think you showed bad judgment," he replied.

In my mind, I pointed out that I had tried to abort the trip when I first saw the "river," but his judgment had prevailed. I also pointed out to myself that I had followed *his* instructions when we had to leave the river. But I'm not sure I made these arguments in his office. He outranked me, and I didn't see what I could accomplish by trying to show that the bad decisions were his, not mine. Nor did I see what could be done about it—the trip was a fiasco, but it was over and not likely to be repeated. Besides, the astonishing deadfall would make for quite a story, and if my film came out, quite a photograph.

Thinking about it today, I realize that *most* of my canoe trips have been fiascos, but all of them are over. Nobody died. And they all make good stories—perhaps also cautionary tales with wisdom for future generations of paddlers. I tell fourteen of them in this little memoir, which will also include some reflections about my life beyond paddling.

The only wisdom I could draw from this tale was, however: No matter what its name, never canoe a body of water so narrow that you have to paddle on land. And I suppose we might also conclude, if you're paddling hard and getting nowhere, sometimes the river is at fault, not you.

Notes

1   In later years, the Boy Scouts of America (BSA) became controversial, charged with militarism, nationalism, homophobia, and, paradoxically, failing to protect Scouts from homosexual predators. As this book went to copyediting, the BSA declared bankruptcy. Hence I have not the time, nor is this the place, to treat these complex issues. I remain glad to have experienced Scouting.

2   Technically it's only a "subcontinental divide," because the Gulf of Mexico eventually connects with the Atlantic.

3   This happened 56 years ago, so I'm not certain it was the East Branch of the Presque Isle River.

4   The drawing is based on a photo I took at the time, which I still have.

Skunked by Girls

Although the Service Department was the largest part of the Canoe Base staff, it had the lowest status. Consider my own first job, dishwashing. Although I replaced my "Dishwasher" sign with "Ceramic Sanitation Engineer," it remained the least prestigious job in camp, save only for the poor guy who cleaned the latrine—also in the Service Department, of course.

Members of the Training Department considered themselves the elite. They knew the right way to cook in a Dutch oven. They showed campers the right way to tie up food packs, so that varmints didn't get into them. And of course, they knew how to canoe *right*!

Lean forward to dip the paddle in the water. Your top hand pushes from the chin. It never rises above the level of your nose. Don't ever bend the elbow of your bottom arm. Lean back as you stroke. Keep your blade moving close to the canoe and parallel to it. Then don't waste energy; bring your paddle back up to the front just inches above the water, feathered (blade parallel to the water) to avoid wind resistance. In the stern, don't rudder, use the J-stroke to counteract the tendency of the canoe to turn away from the side on which you're paddling. Never use the "Canadian racing stroke" (with which we were only vaguely familiar anyway). It wastes energy, lifting your top hand high above your head, and can never be maintained over any distance.

Trainers had no knowledge of whitewater techniques,

which made sense, because we had no white water. Rivers in the north country flowed, but the land was too flat to create actual rapids. Later, this gap in my own knowledge would prove troublesome.

Trainers also had the social power to break their own rules when they wished. For example, they taught campers not to go barefoot, a teaching that I'm sure resulted from repeated injuries from stepping on pointed sticks and sharp shells. But trainers had a tradition of wearing moccasins, a Boy Scout product that could be made from a kit in half an hour but that quickly wore through in the sole. Thus, they were going barefoot, their moccasin tops barely held on by bits of leather crossing under the arch. But this only showed their toughness, so nobody enforced the barefoot rule on *them*.

My fourth summer, some members of the training department had become friends with staff members at Camp Manito-wish, our big rivals, located on a different lake about six miles west. They had two separate camps—one male, one female—but the girls' camp was the focus of our energy. Sometimes their groups got to "our camp-sites" (all owned by the State of Wisconsin, of course, or by private landowners) first, and in other ways they bothered us. Probably their existence itself bothered us—after all, wilderness canoeing was a man's enterprise.

So, it happened that our training staff challenged theirs to a race, on our lake, beautiful White Sand Lake. Our train-ers chose their two best teams—maybe they held qualifying heats, I don't know. The day came. Late in the afternoon, their van drove up with four girls (that's what we called them, then) in swimsuits, friends to cheer them on, and two canoes with paddles and life jackets. Most of our staff strolled down to the beach to watch. We had set up a three-legged course: outbound from the swimming area, then right to go around a buoy, then back home.

The four canoes lined up. There wasn't much tension. The Training Staff knew they were going to win. After all, this was long before Title IX. Girls didn't participate in sports in high school back then. They were cheerleaders. Nor did they have teams in college, except maybe in faux sports like synchronized swimming. Besides, boys were bigger. Stronger. What could possibly go wrong?

At the call of "Ready, set, go!" the canoes jumped ahead. Or rather, two of them did. Ours seemed becalmed by comparison. The boy teams got alarmed. They pushed really *hard* from the chin, leaned back *hard* on the stroke, feathered really *well* on the return. The girls took a huge lead. They

were using the Canadian racing stroke, of course.[1] They kept *both* arms straight. Mostly they twisted their torsos, lifting their paddles well above the water, plunged their paddles in, then rotated their bodies the other way, letting their strong abdominal muscles do the work. They didn't give a damn how or if they feathered, and they completed three strokes while our boys finished just two.

Desperate, our trainers tried to emulate the girls, but they were now so far ahead it was hard to copy them. Besides, though it may not be rocket science, the Canadian racing stroke cannot be learned on the fly, so our teams could not catch up. They slunk to the finish line in third and fourth places. The girls had skunked us thoroughly.

Some of us in the Service Department, who had never been convinced of the dogma that the Canadian racing stroke was useless, secretly gloated. I resolved to work on my Canadian racing stroke that summer and have used it some of the time ever since, as a later chapter will tell. I'm sure the girls' example subtly improved my thinking in other ways too. Being canoeing staff, for instance, they were more practiced and more nonchalant than I, service staff, about picking up canoes from the ground single-handed, throwing them over their heads, and carrying them from the water to the canoe trailer. Yet I outweighed and out-sized them by 30% to 50%. I think this example helped me expect equal physical performance from girls and women; I had always expected equal intellectual performance.

Notes

1   The Canadian racing stroke does not seem to be well described on the web, at least not in 2020. If you can't figure it out from the next sentences, stop by my house and I'll show it to you.

Further Reflections on Girls, Boys, and Sports in the Olden Days

I realize I should not pass so cavalierly over this triumph by what was then called, even in everyday discourse, "the weaker sex." Title IX and the feminist movement have brought to pass a revolution in our views—everybody's views—of what girls can do and what is proper for girls (later "women") to do.

Back when girls won this victory on White Sand Lake, they hardly played any sports, at least not on organized high school or college teams. One exception in some parts of the country was something called "girls' basketball," played by six-girl teams. Three on each team played "guard," in the backcourt, three played "forward," and nobody could cross the center line! This meant that six players were always resting, which we were told was appropriate, lest the females get too tired. Only forwards could score. The result was a strange-looking game with six girls lined up at the centerline, yelling for the ball or trying to intercept it. Also, players could only dribble twice (later made thrice), which eliminated the fast break, again because running hard was improper for girls.

Mostly, instead of playing team sports themselves, girls were cheerleaders and pom-pom girls, cheering for the boys' teams.

When I started teaching introductory sociology to my classes of maybe 150 students at the University of Vermont in 1975, I used a gimmick to open my mini-unit on gender:

I gently tossed (overhand) a tennis ball to a woman student in the middle of the auditorium. Usually, not always, she caught it. Then I asked her to throw it back. Often she failed: the ball never even reached the stage. Even when it did, the throw was usually weak and ineffectual, coming in at ankle level and causing snickers in the room. I would ask a male student why he was laughing, and he would reply, "She throws like a girl."

That was true. She did. When I became a parent, first of a boy, then a girl, I quickly realized that many, perhaps most, toddlers throw "like girls," leading with their elbow and not stepping forward with their opposite foot. Throwing, like most human activities, is learned, and I made sure that *both* of my children threw "like boys," or, shall we say, correctly.

Not only was it a lack of learning. Women were not supposed to do anything as hard as they could. Doing so wasn't "ladylike." This hit me upside the head when the adult volleyball league in which I played engaged two members of the UVM girls volleyball team to teach a workshop on basic skills and rules. The first exercise they led us through required us to strike the ball as hard as we could down to the floor in front of us on an angle so it would then hit the wall and bounce back to us. Of course, they demonstrated it first, and their contact with the ball resounded through the gym like beaver tails hitting the Winooski River at dusk. I realized I had rarely heard girls—still the term used at UVM in the '70s—do anything that made much noise.

The advent of girls' teams—in particular softball—helped girls throw better. Other parents must have been teaching their daughters how to throw, as well. By 1985, I gave up my classroom exercise, because at least half of my women students threw the ball back to me just fine. But remember, at Canoe Base those girls from Camp Manito-wish had skunked us in about 1963.

Even today, women rarely beat men in "men's sports."

Women golfers use shorter tee grounds. Women tennis stars play only until one person has won two sets; men play until one has won three. There are physiological reasons why most men golfers can outdrive most women golfers and why most men tennis stars can beat most women tennis stars. But there are no physiological reasons why male tennis stars play best of five sets while females play best of three. That's an atavism—a holdover from a previous and more primitive era.

As I was writing this reflection in 2019, I attended a formal luncheon at the University of Vermont. Our round table of eight included three women, and the waitress made a point of serving them first.[1] Why? Because that's simply how we did things in, say, 1963, and for that matter, probably in 1863. As the owner of more than 120 fine dining (not merely eating) establishments put it, "there are generations of history behind it."[2] The women don't really get a head start, because we are all supposed to wait until everyone is served before anyone begins to eat. The problem is: the practice calls attention to a distinction that does not need emphasizing. After all, men and women at lunch do exactly the same thing: eat. Indeed, at the UVM luncheon, we all ate the same Chicken Kiev.

I used the term "waitress" above. I did have reason to use it, because I wanted you to know it was a female waiter. But otherwise surely we should say "waiter." Again, why call attention to gender when male and female waiters do exactly the same thing? If you're not convinced, or if you want to hold out for "wait staffer," consider "poetess." Once in widespread use, it still is not listed as "archaic"; dictionaries simply define it as "a woman who writes poetry." That seems perfectly straightforward, until you realize that a man who writes poetry is called a "poet."

"Poet" is no longer gendered. The "poet laureate" of the United States does not become the "poetess laureate" when a woman wins the honor. At Wikipedia, "poetess" redirects to "poet." Why then is "waiter" still considered male, while "poet" is not? And what about "actress"? Male and female actors do exactly the same thing. Why divide them by gender? Again, we must degender our language so "actor" no longer implies male.[3] Surely we shall not substitute "act staff"! Hence retaining "actress" implies that the main actors, the real ones, are male. That won't do![4]

Although this essay has focused on canoeing, throwing, and volleyball, sports are always symbolic of larger societal issues. Another example from my 1975 introductory sociology class brought this home to me. I had just become a single father. On two occasions, when South Burlington schools had closed owing to "teacher in-service days," I had brought my five-year-old son Nick to class, having no other good childcare alternative, so my students knew I had childcare responsibilities.[5] Nevertheless, when we launched into our main treatment of gender roles, two women hijacked the discussion by saying, vehemently and almost in unison, "It's wrong to try to balance motherhood and a career." A male student timidly asked, "But what if you really *want* to be a doctor, or a lawyer, or something else?" "Then *don't have kids!*" came the reply in unison.

I stood right there, in the front of the room! How could they ignore my existence? Because *mothers*, not parents, had children back then. It wasn't until 2018 that General Mills updated its trademarked slogan for Kix cereal from "Kid-tested. Mother-approved." to make it "Parent-approved."

Even today, the use of "parent" is often only cosmetic. In 2018, for example, an issue of *Parents* magazine had just 2 photos of dads only, 5 of both genders, and 28 showing only moms. Issues in 2019 proved similarly skewed. *Parents* is really intended for mothers, as sometimes slips out, such as when they title an article, "Good Stuff: Must-Haves and Must-Dos for Mom and Family." An article on when families should buy organic foods gets called "The Realist Mom's Guide to Organics." But dads purchase groceries too!

Erasure of fathering is deep in our culture. In 2020, I asked Maceo, my nine-year-old grandson, to comment on five children's stories I had written. Each ended with a little boy being put to bed by his mother. My son, Maceo's dad, had done about 60% of the parenting, partly because his job—teacher in an independent high school—involves less structured time than their mother's job. So I asked Maceo if I should change "mother" to "father" at the end of each story. "That would make it weird," he replied. Should I do so in half of the stories? I asked. No, he replied. "Normally in books the mother's at home and the dad's at work." Ironically, his own experience didn't matter; the "shoulds" are in our culture.

The girls of Camp Manito-wish, with their Canadian racing stroke, were actually way ahead of their time.[6] We still have a long way to go to become a society that is not taken aback when dads buy food or girls win canoe races.

Notes

1   At first I didn't believe it, then I recognized the pattern. It turns out to be common practice still, at fine dining establishments, and the only reason I was surprised is that I usually *eat* out, rather than *dine* out, if you get my drift. At Popeye's you pick up your food yourself, and even at elegant places like Applebee's and Olive Garden, the waiters serve everyone in order quickly.

2   Kevin Brown, quoted in Phil Vettel, "Ladies First (Except When It's Not)," *Chicago Tribune*, November 13, 2008, https://www.chicagotribune.com/news/ct-xpm-2008-11-13-0811110152-story.html.

3   Hopefully, the under-twenty crowd is already making this change.

4   Similarly, "sculptress" is on the way out; Google delivers at least 100 times more hits for "sculptor" than "sculptress." The Museum of Women in the Arts in Washington DC, a feminist institution under women's control, calls female sculptors "sculptors," as it should.

5   He sat quietly in a far corner of the lecture hall and amused himself with a book and a toy.

6   It's beginning to happen in wrestling, where weight classes help
     equalize the genders. See Liz Clarke, "A North Carolina Girl Won
     a State Wrestling Title and 'Inspired a Lot of Kids,'" *Washington
     Post*, February 29, 2020, https://www.washingtonpost.com/
     sports/2020/02/29/north-carolina-girl-won-state-wrestling-title-
     inspired-lot-kids/.

Skunking the Girls

It fell to the Service Department to avenge Canoe Base's honor. That summer, a skunk took up residence under the dining hall. This was OK; we had a live-and-let-live philosophy regarding nature and had taken pride in the small extended family of bats that roosted in the eaves of our trading post. But then, several times, our skunk and our year-round caretaker's dog had surprised each other at dawn at an opening to the crawl space under the dining hall. You cannot imagine how unappetizing oatmeal can be when consumed in the atmosphere of intense skunk smell.

Something had to be done.

A member of the Service Department, whom I will call John (because that was his name), knew what to do. He said he could run down the skunk and grab him by the tail. I have forgotten how John knew this—had he seen it done? Heard about it? This was half a century before the internet, so he didn't consult a video!

I signed on to help. After supper, at dusk, when the skunk was likely to be out and about, we gathered our materials: the camp "Brown Duck," an old carry-all truck that the Scouts had gotten free from Army Surplus, a garbage can with lid, and a pair of work gloves. Sure enough, we spotted the skunk some distance behind the dining hall, and John ran after her. (Him? We never checked.) Skunks must have time to plant both feet to spray, it turns out, and with John running, she didn't have a chance. John swooped down a

gloved hand, grabbed the tail, and held his arm straight out from his body.

Some animals are agile enough to curl up and bite whoever is holding them, but skunks cannot do this, so she just hung from her tail. Skunks cannot spray unless they have both feet firmly planted on the ground, I knew, but then I saw her planting her feet in midair, preparing to spray him. I called to John to wiggle her, which he did, so she could not spray. Meanwhile, he was coming to me at a fast walk. I was bringing the metal garbage can. I took off the lid, John dropped in the skunk, and I put the lid back on. Then we carried the can to the Brown Duck.

John rode in the back with the can, keeping it upright and lidded, while I drove straight to Camp Manito-wish. I turned into their private drive, drove most of the way to the property, and turned the truck around. Then John and I got the garbage can down from the truck, set it on the ground, tilted it toward the camp, and took off the lid. The skunk got out and sauntered down the road toward the camp.[1]

We made a clean getaway. If it's too much to claim that we redeemed Canoe Base's honor, we can at least say that we skunked Camp Manito-wish.

But that was not quite the end of the tale. Almost six decades later, as I was working on these stories for publication, I had lunch with Wendell, an old friend from Canoe Base days, now a high executive in the University of California system. Our conversation wandered to old times, and he told me an interesting story about how John caught a skunk at Canoe Base.

Our stories had the same starting point: staff annoyance at the skunk that had taken up residence under the dining hall. Both of us featured John in the starring role, although Wendell remembered John more harshly than I did, as a sort of braggart know-it-all. Anyway, as Wendell told it, John caught the skunk by the tail, which Wendell learned only when John brought him (or her) into the staff living quarters, brandishing it for all to see. "Get that outta here!" was Wendell's reply, and Wendell then got the Brown Duck and drove John and the skunk to the Boulder Junction town dump.

Wendell was weak on details. For example, how had John caught the skunk? What did he do with it while Wendell got the truck? What did he do with the skunk *in* the truck? But it was fascinating to me to listen to an alternative version of a story that in reality featured *me*—at least in my version!

Notes

1   Skunks always seem to saunter. I think they over-rely on their scent as license to saunter, and this story should give them something to think about.

A Further Reflection:
Oral History Is More Accurate
Than Written Sources When
the Topic Is Shameful

At this point, we need to consider the matter of oral history more fully. To a sociologist, the position of oral history within the historical profession is curious. Often historians marginalize oral history as inferior to written sources; sometimes they flatly call oral sources untrustworthy. Historian Donald C. Swain agrees with this criticism: "Oral history is a subject on which American historians are astonishingly uninformed. . . . As graduate students, we are taught to rely primarily on the written record and to question the credibility of word-of-mouth evidence."[1]

Here is an ironic example of the problem: Introducing Herbert Aptheker's *Documentary History of the Negro People in the United States, 1910-1932*, historian Charles H. Wesley writes, "Documents are the historical sources and traces which have come to us out of the past through the thoughts, words, and actions of men and women in their times." He concludes, "No documents, no history."[2] This is particularly ironic because teaching slaves to read and write was a felony in most states.

To sociologists, all this is nonsense. Talking with people is the most common method we use. If we want to learn whether males or females are more favorable toward gay marriage, for example, we ask them. Moreover, sociologists realize that most written materials originated orally, so the idea of distinguishing oral and written sources to privilege the latter is misguided from the start.

I must confess an interest here: I premiered my 2005 book, *Sundown Towns*, in my hometown of Decatur, Illinois. This was appropriate, because a Decatur audience provided me with a breakthrough moment when I was writing about these all-white towns and counties.[3] Hence the very first public mention of the book appeared in my hometown newspaper, the *Decatur Herald & Review*. It was titled "Critics Attack Research of Author in Racism Book," instead of being a puff piece for a local author who made good. The attack was on my reliance on interviews with residents, officials, and historians of sundown towns, instead of written sources. In particular, the reporter critiqued my claim that Villa Grove, a small town between Decatur and Champaign/Urbana, sounded a siren at 6:00 p.m., originally to warn African Americans to leave. I based this claim on a total of nine conversations with residents of Villa Grove and two with residents of nearby towns. Nevertheless, the reporter talked with a professor at the nearby University of Illinois "who has edited or written eight books" and who said, "I want a document." The reporter neglected to mention that the professor specialized in medieval French history. I must admit that I also would not use oral history to study medieval France. The reporter also failed to disclose that he himself lived in Villa Grove.[4]

I tell the story of Villa Grove's siren in *Sundown Towns*, so I'll not repeat it here, but I shall recount the last conversation I had in Villa Grove. It was with the staff of the town's weekly newspaper. I had deliberately saved it until last, because I knew that some small-town editors don't want to print or admit anything negative about their communities. I went into the storefront office of the *Villa Grove News*, which looked like a Hollywood set for a newspaper published in 1890. I told the editor that I was researching towns in Illinois that had a history of keeping out African Americans. He nodded, so I asked, "Tell me the story about the siren on the water tower."

"I don't know any story about that siren," he replied.

I didn't believe him, but I could hardly argue that he *did* know it, so I simply said "Thank you" and turned to leave. At this point, his administrative assistant, who was also at the front counter, said, "Do you mean the story that it sounded at 6:00 p.m. to tell blacks to be out of town?"

"Yes, *that* story," I replied.

"I never heard *that* story!" she then said.

I managed not to laugh until after I got out of the office and around the corner, but her remarks encapsulated the problem: no documentation of Villa Grove's siren will ever surface in Villa Grove, if the editor has his way. For that matter, very little evidence of anything will see print, because in August 2019, the newspaper closed. The town now has to rely on a Villa Grove edition of the nearby *Tuscola Journal*.

Oral history as a field is usually said to have begun in 1948, when Allen Nevins started it at Columbia University. Actually, it dates back millennia. The US Census, perhaps the ultimate written source, relied on an enumerator standing at the front door, talking with the householder, from its beginning in 1790. Most newspaper articles begin when a reporter talks with someone about what happened. Public opinion surveys start with phone calls. Court stenographers transcribe oral testimony.

When the topic is shameful or controversial, oral sources are typically *more* accurate than written sources. An archivist at the National Baseball Hall of Fame and Museum and a librarian at its Giamatti Research Center both told me that you cannot prove that Major League Baseball excluded African Americans before 1947 based on documents. Tell that to Jackie Robinson! Tell it to the St. Louis Cardinal players who threatened to strike if Robinson played in Sportsman's Park.[5] Absence of evidence is not evidence of absence, especially when oral histories supply overwhelming evidence.

Sundown Towns relied substantially on what historians would call oral history. These towns determined—formally or informally—to be all-white, mostly during the "Nadir of race relations," between 1890 and 1940. The term "sundown town" arose from the signs that some communities placed at their railroad stations or city limits, typically saying "Nigger, Don't Let The Sun Go Down On You In Manitowoc," as was posted at that Wisconsin city's limits into the 1960s.

By the 1990s and 2000s, many towns and counties that formerly excluded African Americans came to admit them. Many residents now regretted their towns' racist pasts. Yet some communities still display second-generation sundown town problems such as all-white teaching staffs, all-white police forces, and racist rhetoric. For these and other reasons, it remains important to confirm sundown policies even in towns that have moved beyond them.

Oral history offers the best way to do this. As with Major League Baseball, few written sources exist. I have sought them diligently. In town after town whose oral histories confirm with details that they "boasted" sundown signs at their city limits, I have asked librarians and local historians, "Did you preserve the sign? Did you save any photograph of the sign?"

"Why on earth would we keep *that*?" they reply.

"Because it documents an important aspect of your town," I want to respond, but my job is to find out what they *did* keep, not harangue them about what they threw away.

In 2002 I sent letters to fifty historical societies in probable sundown towns across Pennsylvania, asking if they had written evidence *or oral tradition* that their communities had been unwelcoming to African Americans. Only seven replied at all, and all of those wrote, "We have no documentation that [our town] fits the parameters you describe." Notice how this reply finesses the issue of oral evidence.

Interviewed face to face, historical society members

are often more forthcoming. Of course, talking with me is safer than writing or emailing: no neighbors can ever learn for sure who told me what.

Here is an example, ironically from my hometown, of how talking with people can confirm an all-white town as a sundown town. In October 2001, I keynoted the second Decatur Writers Conference, because my book, *Lies My Teacher Told Me*, made me the third-best-selling author from Decatur.[6] I talked about *Lies* and its sequel of sorts, *Lies across America*. At the end of my talk I explained what I was now working on—*Sundown Towns*—and invited anyone with knowledge of such practices to come down and talk with me. To my astonishment, more than twenty people came to the front and told me about most of the small towns around Decatur. Growing up in Decatur, I had known these places were all-white, but it had never occurred to me that they might be all-white on purpose. I thought black folks were simply displaying good judgment by avoiding dinky little places too small to have a movie theater. Now, audience members confirmed town after town with details. Two people told me, for example, that Niantic, a town of 890 people just northwest of Decatur, had a sundown ordinance, making it illegal for African Americans to be within the city limits after dark. They went on to say that when the Wabash Railroad's work trains were in the Niantic part of its huge yard as dusk approached, they pulled them into the Decatur part of the yard. Workers, including black track layers, slept on the work train, and the Wabash did not want to run afoul of the ordinance. I spoke later with two retired employees of the Wabash, who agreed that they did follow that practice. So I now had four different people who had told me of Niantic's ordinance and how it was indeed obeyed. I considered Niantic confirmed. I still do.

Largely based on oral history, my book confirmed hundreds of towns across the United States. To date, only one has been revealed to be a false positive: Buffalo, a hamlet just east of Springfield, Illinois. Ironically, a written source—a 1908 story in the *Chicago Tribune*—told that whites drove out its black population in the aftermath of the Springfield race riot, itself an attempt to turn the state capital into a sundown town. Historians have quoted this article widely since then. But the *Tribune* reporter never left Springfield. As a consequence, he got the story wrong. Whites threatened and drove out African Americans from Dawson, three miles nearer to Springfield, not Buffalo. The reporter got confused because the white hunting club that made the threat in Dawson was indeed the Buffalo Sharp Shooters, but it was named for the animal, not the town. Even more ironic, I learned of the mistake through oral history. An African American woman who grew up in Buffalo attended a talk I gave at Illinois State University in nearby Normal. Afterward she convinced me Buffalo had never been a sundown town by driving me around the town and introducing me to her relatives who still lived there.

To be sure, memory can be unreliable. But so can be documents. "Interrogate the document," historians cry, by which they mean ask searching questions of it. Indeed, that is good practice, but as Socrates noted some time ago, "If you ask a piece of writing a question, it remains silent." People, on the other hand, talk back. Misunderstandings can be fixed. Wrong information can be corrected.

About the two conflicting skunk stories, I *was* able to "interrogate" Wendell. He replied. Eventually, he agreed ambiguously that my version was correct.

Lord Acton famously said, "History . . . must stand on documents, not on opinions." He *should* have said "must stand on evidence," not "documents." And sometimes— when the topic is reprehensible—the best evidence may be oral.

Notes

1   Swain, "Problems for Practitioners of Oral History," *American Archivist*, no. 1 (January 1965): 63.

2   (Secaucus, NJ: Citadel, 1973), ix, xi. Ironically, Aptheker was a leader in finding sources from which the views of those who left no documents—including illiterate enslaved African Americans—could be inferred.

3   The breakthrough was my realization that *most* towns in Illinois, not just a few, were all-white on purpose.

4   Huey Freeman, "Critics Attack Research of Author in Racism Book," *Decatur Herald & Review*, September 16, 2005. In a further irony, the historian felt free to critique my methods based solely on the reporter's oral description of them, even though he had available to him the whole document—my book *Sundown Towns*.

5   On a topic related to mine, historian Lawrence Goodwin made this point in "Populist Dreams and Negro Rights in East Texas as a Case Study, *American Historical Review* 16, no. 5 (December 1971). He found no written coverage of the racial events he investigated and relied on oral history. Historian Paul Thompson noted that Goodwin's decision to rely on oral history, absent newspaper coverage, "is however rare." "Problems of Method in Oral History," *Oral History* 1, no. 4 (1972): 1.

6   My hosts did not engage Decatur's second-best-selling author, historian Stephen Ambrose, because, as one put it, "He charges $40,000 plus a private jet both ways." I replied, "I saved you more than $37,000!" He agreed.

Abraham Lincoln's Failure, and Ours

After a couple of years on the Canoe Base staff, I wanted more. I wanted to paddle a river in Illinois, where I lived. After all, the Illinois state song, which I had memorized as part of the fifth-grade curriculum, begins:

> By thy rivers gently flowing, Illinois, Illinois,
> O'er thy prairies verdant growing, Illinois, Illinois

I wanted to paddle those rivers—at least the one that flowed through my hometown about half a mile from my house. I lived in Decatur, right in the center of the state, located on the banks of the Sangamon River.

Unfortunately, the Sangamon is about as different from the rivers near Canoe Base as is possible on this earth. Rivers in Wisconsin and the Upper Peninsula of Michigan flow (when beavers haven't dammed them). Illinois rivers look stationary. That's because they are. Geographers define "stream slope" as "rise over run" and measure it in feet of rise (going upstream) per thousand feet of distance. Northeast of Decatur, the Sangamon rises just over two *inches* per thousand feet.[1] Flow is hard to discern.

I wrote part of this story while at a "White Privilege Conference" in Cedar Rapids, Iowa. The Cedar River indeed flows swiftly through the city, right at the edge of downtown, justifying its name. If early Illinois pioneers had chosen to name Decatur for its river, they would have been forced to call it "Sangamon Slows."

Every river, even the Sangamon, has a poet laureate, however. The Sangamon's, John Knoepfle, manages to make something lyrical of this flow problem: in "At the Sangamon Headwaters," he tells of an aged snapping turtle who "is the wise one he knows which way the river runs."[2] It's not always possible to tell from the bank.

Northern rivers are clear. Illinois rivers are described as "turbid" in polite society. (We call them "muddy.") The Sangamon's turbidity is the color of milk chocolate.

The landscape in central Illinois has been described as "industrialized"—not owing to industry, although Decatur had plenty of that, at least when I was growing up. Rather, row crop farming has industrialized the land itself. Except for the valleys of rivers and creeks, by which I mean the *immediate* river valleys—ten or twenty feet on each side—almost no nature remains in central Illinois. Everything is straight lines. You can drive a mile east of Decatur, lash your steering wheel so it cannot move, and you will wind up in Indianapolis, 150 miles due east. Every mile, there is another crossroads. Every road runs north–south or east–west. Boy Scout hikes were incredibly boring, because no matter how long the hike—twelve, even twenty-one miles—we could always see our destination ahead when we started. It just slowly grew bigger.

The land around Decatur was described rather well by two men at the "Transfer House," the ornate more-or-less round building in Lincoln Square, downtown, where we waited for city buses. One evening in June or July of 1958, when I was sixteen, I was waiting to catch a bus home. Two men sitting next to me had this conversation, which made such an impression on me that I committed it to long-term memory. They were both white, maybe late fifties. I'll call them Red and Fred.

Red: "Lotta corn comin' up."
Fred agrees: "*Lotta* corn comin' up."
Red (aware that he has said something profound): "*Lotta* corn comin' up."
They sit in thoughtful silence a few moments.

Red: "Lotta *beans* comin' up."
Fred agrees: "*Lotta* beans comin' up."
Red: "Lotta beans comin' up."
They sit in silence a few moments.

And then, I swear to God:
Red: "Lotta corn *and* beans comin' up."
Fred: "*Lotta* corn and beans."

Indeed, a lot of corn and beans *were* coming up. In the 1920s, when Lake Decatur was created, about 44% of its watershed was in row crops, mostly corn. But by 1958, when this conversation took place, corn and beans took up 85% of all the land that flowed into the Sangamon and then into the lake. Grassy crops like oats and wheat decreased to zero while soybean acreage exploded. All other human and natural activity—other crops, pastureland for livestock, roads, towns, industry, houses, schools, businesses, and parking lots—got crammed into the remaining 15%.[3]

Even the radio station was WSOY!

This astounding concentration into row crops meant that when rain fell, it ran off straight into the Sangamon. It had no woods or wetlands or meadows to soak into. As it ran off, it had no time to lose the contaminants it had gathered—the silt, fertilizer, parking lot runoff, and other pollutants. Everything went into the river.

In 1922, Decatur had dammed the Sangamon about a mile from my house to form Lake Decatur. It supplied Decatur's water and was also supposed to be a recreational amenity. But the saying about the lake was, "too thick to swim in, too thin to plow." As a lad, I did swim at the "beach," which Decatur had created by trucking in loads of sand from nearby sand and gravel pits and spreading it along the shore at a city park. After each swim, however, you would have a silt line horizontally across your face halfway between your lower lip and your chin. You simply *had* to shower.

The lake was also problematic as a water source. The industrial farming practices include heavy application of nitrate-based fertilizers, which resulted in excessive nitrate levels in the Sangamon River and eventually in Decatur's tap water. Many times the city has had to warn people not to allow babies to consume water in Decatur because of "blue baby syndrome." Personally, I too try to avoid foods and water that are forbidden to babies and pregnant mothers. Decatur had the worst concentration of nitrates of any place in the state and probably the nation.

The situation has not improved. A 2010 EPA report says Lake Decatur is plagued by: excess algae, excess sediment, low oxygen, metals, murky water, nitrogen and phosphorus, PCBs, and pesticides. The EPA lists the Sangamon as "polluted," owing to fecal coliform and PCBs. People must avoid touching the river (owing to the first) and avoid eating fish from it (owing to the second).

This was the river I planned to paddle.

To be fair, the Sangamon was better known than rivers

like the Presque Isle and the Manitowish. Indeed, Abraham
Lincoln had made the Sangamon modestly famous, because
at the tender age of 22—my age then exactly!—he canoed
down it from his father's home just west of Decatur to
Springfield, the state capital. In his own words, writing
about himself in the third person, Lincoln told the story:

> Abraham, together with his stepmother's son, John
> D. Johnston, and John Hanks, yet residing in Macon
> County, hired themselves to Denton Offutt to take a
> flatboat from Beardstown, Illinois, to New Orleans,;
> and for that purpose were to join him—Offutt—at
> Springfield, Illinois, so soon as the snow should go
> off. When it did go off, which was about the first of
> March, 1831, the county was so flooded as to make
> traveling by land impracticable; to obviate which dif-
> ficulty they purchased a large canoe, and came down
> the Sangamon River in it. This is the time and the
> manner of Abraham's first entrance into Sangamon
> County. They found Offutt at Springfield, but learned
> from him that he had failed in getting a boat at
> Beardstown. This led to their hiring themselves to
> him for twelve dollars per month each, and getting
> the timber out of the trees and building a boat at
> Old Sangamon town on the Sangamon River, seven
> miles northwest of Springfield, which boat they took
> to New Orleans, substantially upon the old contract.[4]

Lincoln never forgot his experience on the Sangamon
and the navigational difficulties he had faced. When he ran
for state legislature in 1832, he proposed a bill to make it
more navigable as a centerpiece of his platform. "The drifted
timber . . . is the most formidable barrier to this project," he
noted. He also proposed cutting through the necks of the
long peninsulas that the river made, which would be easier
than clearing all the deadfalls.[5]

Unfortunately, I had not researched Lincoln's experience on the Sangamon before setting into motion my own. Also, unfortunately, Lincoln lost the election and never got the Sangamon fixed.

I recruited a friend from Decatur who also worked at Canoe Base. We borrowed a canoe from the local Scout camp on Lake Decatur, and he talked his father into driving us to a likely put-in spot where the river crossed a county road northeast of Decatur. Although we couldn't see our destination when we set forth canoeing, we would always know where we were, because the roads were an inch apart on our map and a mile apart on the ground. What could possibly go wrong?

We put in. There seemed to be plenty of water, mud brown, of course. It even seemed to be flowing, at least a little. We paddled for maybe a quarter mile. Then we got into a narrow woods—really just a line of trees on each side of the river. Immediately we encountered Lincoln's "drifted timber"—tree after tree that had fallen entirely across the rather narrow river.

Had we brought a chainsaw, we might have been all right. Alas, we had nothing but our paddles. So we gave up, walked to the nearest farmhouse, and called my father. He drove out to get us while we packed the canoe out to the nearby county road to meet him.

We had traveled perhaps half a mile in all. Moreover, we would have made that distance much faster without the canoe. If only Lincoln had fixed it!

Notes

1   Illinois Office of Sediment and Wetland Studies, "Watershed Monitoring and Land Use Evaluation for the Lake Decatur Watershed," (Springfield: Illinois State Water Survey no. 169, 1996), https://www.isws.illinois.edu/pubdoc/MP/ISWSMP-169.pdf, fig. 6.
2   John Knoepfle, "At the Sangamon Headwaters," *Poems from the Sangamon* (Urbana: University of Illinois Press, 1985), 4.

3   Illinois Office of Sediment and Wetland Studies, "Watershed Monitoring and Land Use Evaluation," figs. 7–13.

4   Abraham Lincoln quoted in Ida M. Tarbell, ed., *The Life of Abraham Lincoln, Vol. One* (New York: Macmillan, 1917), 51–52.

5   Abraham Lincoln, "The Improvement of Sangamon River," in *Early Speeches, 1832-1856* (New York: Current Literature, 1907), 2–7.

Further Reflections on Lincoln in History

When Abraham Lincoln tried to fix the Sangamon, he ran for the Illinois House as a Whig. Whigs believed in government action to improve the nation. Democrats claimed not to.[1] Whigs also differed from Democrats in another important way: they were always moderately less racist, whether the issue was Native American rights, slavery, or Chinese immigration. Lincoln shared these positions, partly because his trip down the Sangamon and eventually to New Orleans gave him a firsthand view of slavery that he never forgot.

Yet today most high school history textbooks take pains to distance Lincoln from any concern about slavery. They do this by quoting, not the Gettysburg Address with its "new birth of freedom," or his Second Inaugural,[2] with its searing long sentences comparing "this mighty scourge of war" to the literal scourging of slaves. No, textbooks' favorite statement by Lincoln is a passage from a letter he wrote on August 22, 1862, to the *New York Tribune*:

> I would save the Union. . . . If I could save the Union without freeing any slave, I would do it; and if I could save it by freeing *all* the slaves, I would do it; and if I could save it by freeing some and leaving others alone, I would also do that. What I do about slavery and the colored race I do because I believe it helps to save this Union; and what I forbear, I forbear

because I do not believe it would help to save the Union.

Moreover, they present these words to convey to students Lincoln's motivation in pursuing the Civil War, in his own words.

With this quote and their discussion of it, our textbooks encourage students to venerate Abraham Lincoln because "he saved the Union." Period. They specifically deny that Lincoln sought to end slavery. As a result, both sides in the Civil War can claim moral equivalence. No one is offended.

This is bad history. To make this claim, textbooks first leave out the political context. Lincoln wrote to seek support for the war from Northern defenders of slavery. New York City then and now was one of the most Democratic jurisdictions in the nation. Democrats then were openly white supremacist—they called themselves "the white man's party" into the 1920s.[3] Lincoln could *never* appeal to New Yorkers to support the Civil War on the basis that it would help end slavery. Such an argument would only intensify their opposition to the war effort. So he made the only pitch he could: support the Civil War to hold the nation together. So would Frederick Douglass have done, had he been president and seeking support from New York City.

Next they leave out the historical context. A month before he wrote the *Tribune*, Lincoln had already presented the Emancipation Proclamation to his cabinet as an irreversible decision, but no textbook notes this when claiming that the Greeley letter is the guide to Lincoln's war aims. Nor does a single textbook tell of Lincoln's encouragement that same summer to a group of abolitionist ministers to "go home and try to bring the people to your views," because "we shall need all the antislavery feeling in the country, and more." If textbooks did, students might grasp how Lincoln, like every political leader, modified his words depending upon his audience.[4] With the ministers, he was cultivating antiracist opposition on his "left," so he could use it to counter Democratic white supremacists on his "right."[5] Surely students would see that indifference was not Lincoln's only response to the issue of slavery in America.

To get their false point about Lincoln across, most textbooks even edit Lincoln's letter to omit his next and final point: "I have here stated my purpose according to my view of *official* duty, and I intend no modification of my oft-expressed *personal* wish that all men, everywhere could be free" (Lincoln's emphasis). That says something very different about Lincoln. So they leave it out.

Saving the Union had *never* been Lincoln's sole concern. After his 1832 "Fix the Sangamon" campaign failed, he ran again for the Illinois House of Representatives in 1834 and won, and in his first year in office, he was one of just five members to vote against a resolution condemning abolitionists.[6] Six years later he took a steamboat down the Ohio River with his best friend, Josh Speed. Years later, when Speed was questioning why Lincoln was becoming a member of the new antislavery Republican Party, he wrote Speed an explanation: "You may remember, as I well do, that from Louisville to the mouth of the Ohio there were on board ten or twelve slaves, shackled together with irons. That sight was continual torment to me, and I see something like it every time I touch the Ohio, or any other slave-border." Lincoln concluded that the memory still has "the power of making me miserable." No textbook quotes this letter. Such a quotation would be simply incompatible with their implied claim that Lincoln did not care about black people or slavery.

To be sure, Lincoln's antiracism was inconsistent. Most of his life, he supported sending African Americans to some foreign haven. Sometimes he pandered to racist audiences.

But in 1860, facing the threat of civil war, he rejected the eleventh-hour Crittenden Compromise, a constitutional amendment seeking to ward off secession by preserving slavery forever and by reenacting the Missouri Compromise line for its expansion. Specifically he used these words: "On the territorial question, I am inflexible. . . . You think slavery is right and ought to be extended; we think it is wrong and ought to be restricted."[7] Near the end of the war, in a speech from the White House balcony on April 11, 1865, Lincoln proposed that at least some African Americans, North and South, should have the right to vote. John Wilkes Booth was in the crowd that night and said to two companions, "That means nigger citizenship. That is the last speech he will ever make. . . . By God, I'll put him through."[8] So Abraham Lincoln was murdered in the cause of white supremacy. Imagine the impact on a young black student of realizing that a white supremacist killed Lincoln! Imagine the impact on a young white student! Yet not one textbook mentions white supremacy or racism as Booth's motivation.

Why might the authors of history textbooks omit such facts? Why is it important to them to concoct a morally indifferent Lincoln? To answer this question, we need to understand that *when* authors wrote about Lincoln influenced *what* they wrote about Lincoln. That is a core insight from historiography—the study of the writing of history.

After 1890, the Confederates—or, more accurately, since it was a new generation, neo-Confederates—won the Civil War. Of course, it ended in 1865. But they won it, or won what it was about, the subjugation of African Americans, in 1890 and the years that followed.

Their victory came in several forms. Late in 1890, white supremacist Democrats in the Senate defeated the Federal Elections Bill, more or less by a single vote. Republicans had put it through the House, and Benjamin Harrison would have signed it into law happily. After the defeat, Democrats responded as they usually did: by tarring Republicans as "nigger-lovers," even using that term. In the past, Republicans had replied, yes, it's an outrage, how you Democrats use violence and fraud in every election against black voters, but in 1891 Republicans made a new response: "No we aren't." So it transpired that during the 1890s, African Americans increasingly found themselves without political allies, hence powerless.[9]

Also in 1890, the US Army committed the massacre at Wounded Knee (South Dakota). Rationalizing this act raised racism toward Native Americans still higher. Worst of all from the standpoint of black civil rights, Mississippi passed its new state constitution, openly barring blacks from voting, office-holding, indeed, from citizenship. Although it flagrantly violated the 14th and 15th Amendments, the US did nothing, encouraging every other Southern state and even Oklahoma to follow suit by 1907.

These three victories for white supremacy set in motion the Nadir of race relations—that terrible era between 1890 and 1940 when racism grew ever stronger, North and South. During the Nadir, neo-Confederates symbolized their victory with Confederate monuments, which went up throughout the South and even as far away as Boston; Madison, Wisconsin; Blaine, Washington; and San Diego.

Neo-Confederates even challenged the name of the war; during the Nadir—and occasionally down to now—it got called "The War Between the States." This is anachronistic; during the war itself, it was called—duh!—the Civil War. I examined the six largest South Carolina newspapers for the period 1860–65 and found not one use of "War Between the States."

Across the North as well as the South, whites increasingly limited the social and legal rights of African Americans during the Nadir. Colleges such as Harvard and the University of Minnesota still let black students attend class but now shut them out of dormitories. Town after town across the West and North went sundown—drove out their black populations, sometimes violently, or took steps to ensure none ever moved in. Chinese Americans, Jews, Native Americans, and Mexican Americans were often likewise targeted. Organizations like the Union League Clubs, founded by Jews as well as Christians, now went anti-Semitic. Eugenics became popular and "scientific."

Consider the situation in Lincoln's hometown on the Sangamon. In 1908 a white mob tried to make Springfield into a sundown town. As they attack black neighborhoods, they yelled, "Abe Lincoln brought you in, and *we* will drive you *out*. Ninety years later, I visited the humble Grand Army of the Republic Museum in Springfield. The GAR was the organization of Union veterans after the Civil War that fought for veterans' benefits and also for Republican principles of interracial justice during Reconstruction. In 1998, when I visited, the only staff member was himself a neo-Confederate! Imagine if a proud descendant of the Waffen-SS staffed a Holocaust memorial museum in Germany![10]

In this cultural climate, Lincoln's very real, though inconsistent, antislavery and antiracist thinking had become an embarrassment. So it had to go. It became unseemly to remember Lincoln for anything *other* than saving the Union. Thus in 1922 the Lincoln Memorial was dedicated in Washington, DC, with the inscription, "In this temple, as in the hearts of the people for whom he saved the Union, the memory of Abraham Lincoln is enshrined forever." Art critic Royal Cortissoz, who wrote it, deliberately omitted slavery: "By saying nothing about slavery," he noted, "you avoid the rubbing of old sores."[11]

Ironically, this Lincoln who did not care about slavery or have much regard for African Americans is also the man whom black nationalists present to African Americans to persuade them to stop thinking well of him. He was merely "forced into glory," as the title of Lerone Bennett's book proclaimed in 2000.[12] Neo-Confederates like James Ronald Kennedy and Walter Donald Kennedy in *The South Was Right!* present the same Lincoln as part of their false argument that secession and the Civil War had little to do with slavery or white supremacy.[13] No wonder that Abraham Lincoln remains little used as an antecedent by today's young people.

Regrettably, if students don't learn about Abraham Lincoln in high school, they will hardly do so afterward; most Americans, even if they go to college, never take a course in US history. Meanwhile, we have conflated his and Washington's birthdays into a single holiday, gradually coming to be called "Presidents' Day," whose main function seems to be to spur retail sales, not to ponder the moral or intellectual legacy of either man. "Presidents' Day" is supposed to honor *all* our presidents, not just the good ones. Buying something on sale might be a rational response to a call to honor the moral and intellectual legacies of, say, James Buchanan or Andrew Johnson.

Thus it can come as no surprise that when I ask college students who their heroes are in American history, only one or two in a hundred pick Lincoln. Even those who do choose him know only that he was "really great"—they don't know why. Their ignorance makes sense—after all, textbooks present him almost devoid of content.

After my Sangamon experience, I cannot recommend that you canoe to Springfield on Lincoln's river. But I do suggest you visit his house, grave, and museum there, and that you revisit his life. Revisit the question, "Was he racist?" I submit that he was, but at other times he was antiracist. Also, consider the refinement, "compared to whom?" To Stephen A. Douglas? Donald J. Trump?

Unfortunately, by suppressing the racism in our past, including Lincoln's, history textbooks make it hard for students to see racism in our present society. And by suppressing the antiracist idealism of Abraham Lincoln, textbooks withhold from students a role model that might inspire them to oppose today's racism, even if they are not perfect on the subject themselves.

Lincoln believed in America because he believed its basic dynamic ultimately stood for true equality of opportunity for all. "It is for us, the living," as he said at Gettysburg, to dedicate ourselves "to the great task remaining before us"—first to putting back into our culture an accurate image of Lincoln's idealism, and then to using it to carry on the unfinished work to achieve social justice which he so nobly advanced.

Notes

1   However, the Democratic Pierce administration completed surely the most important public action on behalf of internal improvements before the Civil War: the Gadsden Purchase, a swath of land bought from Mexico to facilitate a transcontinental railroad from New Orleans to Los Angeles. Jefferson Davis, a traditional Democrat opposed to internal improvements, strongly favored the purchase, since it helped the Southern cause.

2   Eight of the eighteen textbooks I studied for *Lies My Teacher Told Me* do include the Second Inaugural, but seven only quote his "safe" final paragraph, "With malice toward none . . ." Only one includes anything about slavery.

3   In 1920, passage of the 19th Amendment made "man's" anachronistic. "White" didn't really become anachronistic until at least FDR (and Eleanor!).

4   Wouldn't that be a salutary lesson for students to grasp, as they become adults in a world where political leaders *still* say different things to different audiences!

5   Presciently, he also said to them, "When the hour comes for dealing with slavery, I trust I will be willing to do my duty though it cost my life." Which, in fact, it did.

6   He also favored women's suffrage in that early year!

7   Lincoln, letter to John A. Gilmer, Springfield, IL, December 15, 1860.

8   Admiral Porter, *Incidents and Anecdotes of the Civil War* (New York: Appleton, 1886), 295; re Booth, see, inter alia, William Hanchett,

The Lincoln Murder Conspiracies (Urbana: University of Illinois Press, 1983), chap. 2, note 9.

9   Of course, this term rarely saw print. Even in the Lincoln-Douglas debates, attended by stenographers, "nigger" routinely got changed to "negro." Harold Holzer, interview by Brian Lamb, C-Span, July 21, 1993, c-span.org/video/?49145-1/the-lincoln-douglas-debates. Nevertheless, some contemporaneous newspapers do make the point verbatim, including the *Martinsburg* (TN) *Herald,* quoted on the front page of the *Shepherdstown* (WV) *Register* (October 21, 1892); J.F. Stone, "Roast for Republicans," *St. Paul Daily Globe,* May 2, 1894; and "Opening Their Eyes," *St. Landry Clarion* (Opelousas, LA), January 2, 1897. (The *Clarion* mischaracterized the *NY Herald* but makes the point nonetheless.) Cf. Joe B. Wilkins, "The Participation of the Richmond Negro in Politics, 1890–1900," master's thesis, Richmond: University of Richmond, 1972; Donna A. Barnes, *The Louisiana Populist Movement* (Baton Rouge: Louisiana State University Press, 2011), 203–4.

10 For that matter, there *are* no proud descendants of the Waffen-SS in Germany. Having forebears in the Waffen-SS is not something Germans are proud of. Again, that's because the Nazis lost in 1945. Confederates lost in 1865, but then they won in 1890 and after.

11 Scott Sandage, "A Marble House Divided," in R.J. Scott-Childress, ed., *Race and the Production of Modern American Nationalism* (Abingdon-on-Thames: Routledge, 2014), 277–78.

12 Lerone Bennett Jr., *Forced into Glory* (Chicago: Johnson Publishing, 2000).

13 James Ronald Kennedy and Walter Donald Kennedy in *The South Was Right!* (Gretna, LA: Pelican, 1994 [1991]), 26–32. Thomas J. DiLorenzo makes a similar false claim in *The Real Lincoln* (New York: Three Rivers, 2003).

"They're Half an Hour Ahead of You"

After the fiasco of trying to paddle a river in Central Illinois, I was anxious for a more successful canoe trip. As a staff member, I could use a Canoe Base canoe before the season started, so I recruited two Scout friends from Decatur, Joe and Bob, for a three-day canoe trip. Joe's dad let us use his 1960 Volkswagen Beetle. We drove north in June, after our college semesters had ended but before Canoe Base opened.

Since this is a collection of canoeing fiascoes, not driving fiascoes, I won't tell you about how, driving across the flat Illinois prairie in a VW, suddenly I found myself on the shoulder, three feet to the right, because a grain elevator had interrupted the steady crosswind from the right that I had unconsciously been steering into, to stay on the road. But after a day's drive, we reached Canoe Base.

The next morning, we got a canoe, three paddles, two Duluth packs, and life jackets and set forth. First, we paddled the length of White Sand Lake, going west, and then we exited on beautiful White Sand Creek. The creek meandered through a swamp so vividly green that looking at it intensely seemed to hurt. The high grasses hid canoes but sitting canoeists would poke up above. The water was beautifully clear. The switchbacks were so sharp that we could see the next meander a mere football field ahead of us, across the grass, but we had to paddle a quarter mile right and then another quarter mile left to get there.

Soon the creek joined the Manitowish River, which we

paddled upstream, toward the northeast. We pitched camp on the river and cooked up our "Veg-a-Rice" with a small can of chicken for dinner. That night as we went to sleep, we heard the whistling calls of a pair of loons, but we were such city slickers that we didn't know what they were and imagined they were the trumpeting of a moose!

In the morning we portaged to a lake—High Lake, I believe. We continued paddling along this two-mile lake toward the northeast. It was a beautiful day. Across the lake stood a lovely white home, beautifully landscaped with twin pine trees and a flagpole. When we reached the portage take-out near the eastern end of the lake, three fishers were having lunch at a picnic table—two men and a woman. We joined them, ate our sandwiches, and talked about the fishing. Then we set off on the portage to the next lake, two-thirds of a mile toward the northeast.

What you're supposed to do, to portage a canoe, is lash paddles. The training department at Canoe Base had taught us all the right way to lash paddles in a canoe before portaging: lash the blades onto the thwart beyond midship, maybe six inches apart. Lash the shafts off toward the gunwale on each side of the canoe. Then one person carries the canoe, balancing the blades on their shoulders, their hands on the shafts, tilting the canoe up in front to see where they are going.

Lashing paddles takes maybe a full five minutes, however. We thought we'd save that time. We put the paddles in the canoe and loosely tied a "painter" (thin rope) around them so they wouldn't fall out. Then Bob and I positioned ourselves toward the bow and stern and simply threw the canoe over our heads, resting the gunwales on our shoulders, using our hands for relief. Our heads were inside, the canoe was level horizontally, and we couldn't tilt it upward, so we couldn't see a thing except our feet straight down in front of us.

Joe led off our little parade, wearing both backpacks, because he could see where he was going. What could possibly go wrong?

We walked and we walked and we walked and we *walked.* "This is a damn long two-thirds of a mile," I kvetched.

"Well, you are under the canoe," Joe replied. "It seems longer under there."

I figured he must be right. Nevertheless, it was some time later when we finally reached the end of our portage and saw open water again.

We flipped the canoe off our shoulders, which ached for relief, threw the packs in, and set off paddling. Soon I began to feel a sense of déjà vu. "Doesn't this lake look familiar?" I asked.

"How could it?" replied Joe. "We've never been here before. All these Wisconsin lakes look alike."

That certainly sounded reasonable, and we paddled on a while. Then I noticed the house across the lake. Attractive. White. And landscaped with two pine trees and a flagpole. "Do you see that house?" I asked. "That's the same house. The same pine trees. The same flagpole."

Joe had no answer.

"I'm going to look at the map," I said, and stopped paddling to get out the US Geological Survey topographic map of the area. I found our take-out point and the dotted line showing the portage trail to the next lake. I also saw another trail that went off from the portage trail to the left and paralleled High Lake, about a quarter mile to the right of it, for 1.3 miles. Then it turned left and returned to High Lake. Somehow Joe had taken this left turn.

There was nothing to do but paddle back to the same take-out and take the right trail, on to the next lake.

Just now we saw and heard the fishers, in their rowboat, their outboard motor pushing them toward us. The woman sat in front, staring at us, and as they drew closer, we could see the complete consternation that clouded her countenance. And then, suddenly, as if a ray of sunlight hit her face on an overcast day, her confusion vanished, and she smiled. "The other boys are about half an hour ahead of you," she called out to us. "We had lunch with them at the portage."

"Thank you," I shouted back. What else could I say?

Milking the Government

Like many summer camps, Canoe Base got "government surplus"—commodities provided by the US Department of Agriculture. This program was supposed to maintain good prices for farmers' products while helping nonprofit organizations.

Elements of this program still exist, supplying food to daycare centers, senior living centers, the school lunch program, and other institutions. Canoe Base got hundreds of pounds of frozen ground beef, cartons of "instant nonfat dry milk," boxes of butter, sacks of flour, and a product known as "government cheese." This last was a five-pound brick of undetermined origin, colored orange, that today gets its own Wikipedia entry, which says "it consists of a variety of cheese types and other ingredients such as emulsifiers blended together." The entry also notes that "government cheese has been used as a humorous reference by many comedic performers."

We actually had no problem with the cheese. The ground beef was so important to us that I concocted a two-week menu that included ground beef in some form eleven times. Our problem was the milk.

It was a fine powder, pressure-packed into plastic bags inside cardboard boxes. Each box weighed four pounds and made five gallons of "reconstituted milk." Reconstituted it may have been, but milk it was not—at least not milk that any self-respecting lad would ever drink.

The cartons came with instructions stenciled on them, telling us to sprinkle the powder onto cool water and mix thoroughly. Then we were to let it sit for hours, surely to get rid of the smell, which reminded one of a poorly run hospital. "The resulting product," the instructions concluded, "will not be inferior nutritionally to pasteurized skim milk." We thought that language was touchingly honest—no attempt to claim that it might *resemble* pasteurized skim milk.

Pouring it from one container to another from a height of several feet supposedly aerated it, making it more palatable. We never found a palate for which that worked. We could not bring ourselves to serve it to our campers or our staff. We did put it in pancakes, but that hardly dented the many cartons we had.

Fifty years later, the government still distributes this stuff, and it still suggests: "Use nonfat dry milk as directed in recipes requiring dry or reconstituted milk or as a substitute in a cooked product when fresh milk is specified." Perhaps it was a failure of our imagination, but we never came up with a "recipe requiring dry or reconstituted milk." Our cook refused to risk her reputation substituting this powder in water for fresh milk in anything she cooked.

We had lots of boxes. What were we to do?

According to government regulations, we could not sell commodity foods. That would undercut local grocery stores. We could not give them away. We could not even store them over the winter—my predecessor had tried that the previous year, and a USDA inspector had dropped by in February, found the milk, and fined us. All we could do was, turn it back to the government. If we did that, however, according to rumors among other food recipients, the government would not only cut our allotment of milk for the next year but would cut *all* our government surplus proportionately. We could not risk that.

I had a brainstorm. Why not line the volleyball court with it? The twine we were using kept breaking. Marking just the corners led to arguments. So another staff member and I measured carefully and laid out two-inch lines of dried milk on each side of the net.

They worked perfectly, for two days. On the third day, it rained. The lines were still there, a bit yellowed perhaps, but functional. On the fourth day, however, the entire court stank like spoiled milk. Not bad enough to deter play, but it does explain why Wimbledon prefers titanium dioxide.

I had thought we would have to reline at regular intervals, but almost immediately it became clear that we would not. A streak of deep green grass, taller and thicker than the rest, soon grew along every white line we had put down. This richer grass continued to mark the court for the next two summers.

The volleyball court proved the value of milk as fertilizer. Nevertheless, today we have a compost-industrial complex, complete with stainless steel raised canisters (to keep out—ugh!—worms and bacteria), paid gurus, and lists of "thou shalts" and "thou shalt nots." One authority held forth on NPR not long ago. Asked if she was a purist who only made vegan compost, she replied, "Oh, no." She included "crushed eggshells," she went on, although she always rinsed them out first. Presumably unrinsed eggshells might offend the maggots, bacteria, worms, and larvae that convert table scraps to compost.

One of the "thou shalt not" rules is "no dairy." Authority Melinda Myers declared, "No meat, no dairy, no bones, no fat" on NPR in 2019; she also had no data.[1] At our house, we put everything in our compost. Well, almost everything: no bone except fishbones—others take too long to break down—and no industrial "food" like Coca-Cola. Houseguests are horrified. "You put milk in your compost?" one asks, as I rinse my cereal bowl and put the results in the compost can.

"What do cows eat?" I reply. "Ashes to ashes and grass to grass."

Unfortunately, lining the volleyball court used less than two packages' worth of our massive supply. We still faced the problem of what to do with the bulk of our powdered milk. Arlo Guthrie had not yet composed "Alice's Restaurant," but the crime scene in that song (and later the movie)—a roadside dump—was hardly unique to western Massachusetts. I asked two staff members—"Moose" and "Little John"—to take all the rest of our milk to an unofficial dump in a ravine alongside a road along a creek about a mile from Canoe Base. There they were to dump it, but unlike Arlo, they were to leave no incriminating evidence. Instead, they were to bring back every carton, every box, even every plastic bag, for proper disposal. We knew that the serial numbers were traceable. We wanted to bring off the perfect crime.

Moose and John loaded up the "Brown Duck," a vehicle which, like its contraband cargo, was itself government surplus. A carryall painted olive drab, the Army had condemned it years before and given it to the Boy Scouts. Its steering was so loose that in a wide area like a parking lot, the driver could hold the wheel steady and the truck would lurch from left to right as it "caught" first on one side, then the other. Driving in a straight line required a certain Zen-like concentration: one had to anticipate which way it would next lurch and move the wheel several inches to the opposite side until resistance was encountered, then apply a tiny nudge before returning the wheel to the center. I reminded Moose to drive carefully. What could possibly go wrong?

Moose and John returned safely later that afternoon. Someone came to get me at once, so I could behold the sight, and it was unforgettable. At 6'5", Moose was our tallest staff member; at 5'4", John was our shortest. They stood before me, one Mutt, one Jeff, entirely white. It seems that merely slicing open each bag and emptying it into the ravine had grown boring, so they developed a more interesting routine: they whooshed each bag's contents at each other. They now gave new meaning to the term "white folks." Of course their shoes, socks, belts, and all other items of clothing were white. Their skin and hair were perfectly white, everywhere. Their eyebrows were white. Their eye*lids* were white! Even their lips were white.

Their irises and glimpses of their tongues when they spoke provided the only specks of color on their personages.

Fearing prosecution, I've never told this story before. Canoe Base has closed, however, so it is safe from harm. Surely the statute of limitations for violating USDA regulations has expired, so I too can safely tell this tale without legal risk. Nothing can go wrong. And it does have a moral for our time: you can put dairy into compost without fear!

Notes

1   Keeping our sources within Wisconsin, I quote Myers from Joy Powers and Melinda Myers, "Composting Tips & Tricks to Beautify Your Garden," WUWM, October 28, 2019, https://www.wuwm.com/post/composting-tips-tricks-beautify-your-garden#stream/0. The Wisconsin Department of Natural Resources, which developed most of the campsites we used, today provides similar advice to Wisconsin residents: "Add only uncooked vegetable scraps, never scraps containing oils, meats, bones, or dairy products." (DNR: "Home Composting," Madison: Wisconsin Department of Natural Resources, c. 2018, at http://newglarusvillage.com/__media/pdfs/garbage/DNR-The%20Complete%20Composter.pdf. How cooking vegetables might ruin their compost value only data-free gurus know! Cf. Loewen, "The History of Composting in America," History News Network, December 16, 2013, http://historynewsnetwork.org/blog/153202.

A Reflection on Expecting Excellence

Two decades after our milk escapade, I found myself in the company of one of these two staff members at a Christmas party in our mutual hometown of Decatur, Illinois. John and I fondly recounted various Canoe Base stories, but then he took me into a quieter room to tell me something serious. "You were the first person who believed in me," he said. "I was a clown, a fuck-up in high school, but you believed I could do the work at Canoe Base. That changed my life."

I had indeed recommended John for the Canoe Base staff, but I had done so without much thought. He seemed intelligent, energetic, and sunny—and to be sure, I did enjoy his sense of humor. Over the years, a handful of boys had not worked out as staff members, but most had done all right, and I had no doubt that John would fit in.

Unknown to me, my routine recommendation had meant the world to John.

After his success at Canoe Base, John went on to graduate from the University of Illinois and then earn his law degree. When we met that Christmas, he was an established attorney earning a solid income. I didn't think I had made that much difference in his life, but he thought I had.

Since then, talking with first-generation college students in particular, I have come to see how important it is that *someone* believed in them. Otherwise, they were unlikely even to apply to college, and if they did attend, they would doubt that they belonged—the "imposter syndrome." As a result, without some special encouragement, often they failed to graduate.

Most "outsider" students also have to buck a structural problem: so-called standardized tests—the SAT and ACT—tell them that according to science, they do *not* have aptitude for college.

In fact, the SAT and ACT do not measure aptitude. They cannot. Decades ago, Educational Testing Service admitted as much and changed the name of the SAT from "Scholastic Aptitude Test" to "Scholastic Assessment Test" and then to, simply, "SAT." That is, the initials now stand for nothing at all.[1] Nowhere on its home page does "aptitude" appear. But that made no difference. The change proved undetectable to the public. As of 2020, if one Googles "Scholastic Aptitude Test," the SAT website still comes up first, because the phrase is still there invisibly. Naturally people still *think* it stands for aptitude. Consequently, bad SAT scores sap the confidence of many high school students.

I have shown elsewhere how SAT scores vary by region, social class, race, gender, and whether one is rural, urban, or suburban.[2] The SAT does not predict first-semester college grade point well at all, but it does "predict backward" to correlate closely with parental family income. Colleges use it because it's much more defensible to admit richer students owing to their SAT scores rather than simply owing to their incomes. Otherwise, SAT scores are not useful to admissions counselors at most colleges.[3] And they often amount to an additional burden on outsider students, contributing to their self-doubt.

My Christmas conversation with John made me happy. It's always great to learn that you made such a positive impact. The moral I draw from this milk story, in addition to my compost conclusion, is this: expect *a lot* from people who look up to you as a positive role model. Pay attention to their strengths. See if you can discern an attribute worth commending. Then convince them they are able. No one else may be doing this for them, so your expectation may just change their life.

Notes

1   I tell this story in *Teaching What Really Happened* (New York: Teachers College Press, 2009), 55.
2   *Teaching What Really Happened*, 50; "Gender Bias on SAT Items," with Phyllis Rosser and John Katzman, American Educational Research Association, April 1988, New Orleans; ERIC ED294915.
3   Some colleges also worry that if they don't require the SAT, they will not appear to be selective, so better students will not apply. Nevertheless, an increasing number of schools are going "test-optional."

Saved by the Deus

While I was growing up, Gale Brock became something of an older brother to me. He was two years older, and while that might have been a chasm in adolescence, Gale somehow liked being the oldest of a bunch of Boy Scouts.

When I turned fourteen, I became an Explorer Scout. Gale was already one of the leaders of Post Five, which consisted of maybe a dozen boys, ages fourteen through seventeen. The next year, we went to Canoe Base, and Gale was our "voyageur," sent ahead for four days of training so he could lead us for a week of canoe camping on our own.

Gale and I kept up our friendship through college. Among our rituals: every Christmas vacation we got together in Decatur, our hometown, went out to Camp Podesta, the Explorer Scout Camp in a woods twenty miles southeast, and each cooked a steak, using no utensils.

For those who have never done that, you get a young sapling, maybe four or five feet high, choosing one whose future is already limited by its unfortunate placement near a road or next to a larger tree, and break it off. Choose a tree with a Y in its tiny trunk. Break off all the little twigs and branches. Then carefully join the two remaining branches, the Y, to form an oval, like a tennis racket. Twist the skinny ends around each other to lock them in place. Then take the branches you stripped off and clean them of all smaller twigs and branches. Weave them together as you would string the tennis racket—you only need three or four in each direction. You have created a grill.

Build a wood fire. (Boy Scouts are good at that.) If a rock or log is available, put it next to the fire so you can rest the far end of your tennis-racket grill on it. Sprinkle garlic salt heavily on the steak, put it on the grill, and hold it over the fire. The steak will start cooking long before your grill starts burning. (That's why you used a living sapling.)

Use a sharp stick to flip your steak, grill the other side, and retire to your table or log to eat. We always brought along a head of lettuce and a small bottle of salad dressing and ate that too, again without plates or utensils.

One year it was so cold that the lettuce actually froze while we were cooking the steak. But it still tasted OK.

After college, indeed to the end of Gale's life, we stayed friends. This was largely due to his efforts, because I married and had kids and became much more settled. Gale moved to California and took up flying as a hobby. He bought a tiny 1947 Cessna that seated just two people, including the pilot, and one year he flew across the United States in it, seeing friends along the way. Finally he reached me, teaching sociology at the University of Vermont.

He had already done some research on our next step, which of course involved a canoe. We flew to Greenville Municipal Airport next to Moosehead Lake, a huge lake in northern Maine. Moosehead covers almost 120 square miles and has more than 400 miles of shoreline. Gale's plan was to camp right on the airport grounds the first night. The next morning, we would get a ride to town, rent a canoe, paddle across the lake to the wilderness on the eastern shore, put up our tent, and spend the night. The next day we would paddle back, return the canoe, and fly back to Vermont. What could possibly go wrong?

We camped at the airport. That evening, we got a ride to town to see the movie showing downtown. On the way out, a newly made acquaintance tried to get us a ride back to the airport in a friend's car going that way. He yelled at them, but when they didn't hear, he threw his just-purchased ice cream cone at the car. They still didn't notice. I had never seen a more extravagant gesture on behalf of just-met strangers. Then, though it was out of his way, he drove us to the airport. Mainers seemed very nice.

The next day we rented a canoe and paddled up the west side of the lake. My memory of the lake is that it appeared as a sort of figure eight, and we paddled across it at the narrow point, winding up on the eastern shore. Decades later, I cannot now get a map of Moosehead Lake to look like an eight. Maybe we paddled across to Sugar Island. I'm not sure. Certainly there are some campgrounds on that island for canoe campers.

In any case, we enjoyed a beautiful afternoon and evening. We fixed dinner, pitched camp, and talked long into the night.

The next day was another story. It was incredibly windy, and the wind was from the southwest, exactly the direction we had to go. Whipped up by the wind, the whitecaps were huge. Yet we had no alternative: we had no food, we had to return the canoe, and we had lives to get back to in Vermont and California. We had a cold breakfast, but then we had to get moving.

We put our stuff in the canoe, got in, and set forth. But forth, we didn't go. Using the regular paddle stroke, even with perfect feathering, we merely held the canoe steady against the wind. We could paddle all day at that rate, exhaust ourselves, and not advance a single foot!

So we switched to the Canadian racing stroke. Keeping both arms straight, raising our paddles high and swiveling our bodies to get power, we paddled absolutely as hard as we could until exhausted, then pulled onto the shore gasping for breath. Then after a quick respite, we got back into the canoe and repeated the process. We couldn't simply walk along the shoreline pulling the canoe beside us, because the shore dropped off.

An hour of this torture got us up to the point where the lake narrowed. Here we had to cross to the other side. How would we do it? Making a right turn meant the whitecaps would now hit us almost broadside, almost surely swamping us.

As we pondered our dilemma, along came our deus ex machina. A big pleasure boat, already an antique, owned by some Victorian-era lodge on the east side of the lake, came by right in front of us. It was taking a few departing guests across the lake to their cars, picking up new guests, and giving continuing residents an outing on the lake. We hailed it.

The captain, pleased at the diversion we provided to his guests, was happy to take us and our canoe aboard. Twenty minutes later, we docked on the western shore.

Now, if you're like me, you've long known the phrase "deus ex machina," but only vaguely. I knew it referred to a plot twist with no preparation, one that saves the day. But "god from the machine?" What does *that* have to do with the definition? What does it even mean?

"Deus ex machina," although Latin, comes originally from Greeks, indeed, from Greek plays. Often Euripides, who may have invented the device, literally used a machine to bring in a new character or a thing—sometimes the machine itself—to extricate the hero from an impossible situation. Sometimes a trap door brought in the device or actor from the floor; sometimes a crane dropped down from above; usually a Greek god was said to be responsible. In Euripides's *Medea*, a chariot sent by the sun god miraculously carried Medea, who had just committed murder and infanticide, away from her husband Jason to the safety and civilization of Athens.

From ancient times, drama critics have charged that the device is a cop-out, not only used to save the day but also to save the play, when the dramatist could not think of a more plausible way to achieve a happy ending. But here, our savior really *was* a machine, with the godlike power of delivering us across the thundering whitecaps. Moreover, it really happened. Nobody made it up.

I no longer remember how we got back to the airport. I no longer remember our flight home, even though it must have been interesting, flying over the White Mountains of New Hampshire followed by the Green Mountains of Vermont in a 1947 Cessna. The canoe trip was the thing, and the story ended happily, thanks to the deus ex machina.

A Reflection on the Sasha and the Zamani

Gale Brock never married. In about 2005, two decades after our Moosehead Lake adventure, he phoned me from Sacramento, where he lived. He was suffering from non-Hodgkin's lymphoma. Even though we lived 3,000 miles apart, I had been aware of his long decline. He had told me he planned to take his best friend on a farewell trip to a resort town in Mexico where they had had a wonderful time years before, but first he needed to make sure that she would not be embarrassed by his need for a wheelchair in LAX airport. Now on the phone he told me they had taken that trip, and it had been good. Now he was dying, and he wanted to say goodbye to me.

That evening, I don't think I reminded him of our deus ex machina. I'm not sure we talked about canoeing at all. I knew Gale did not believe in God or an afterlife, and I had no certainty on these points to pass on to him. He told me he had some friends over—people I had met on visits with Gale—to say goodbye to them. Later that evening he planned to end his life. He had his own deus ex machina, a pistol he had owned for many years, and he planned to send his friends out for coffee and then shoot himself in the heart. When they returned they would find his body. That way none of them could get in trouble for assisted suicide.

It sounded rational to me, not suicide at all, merely a matter of timing. He had now found it impossible to live outside of a hospital. In a later chapter I call this a Niagara death. I was very sad and told him so, but I wished him well.

To my surprise, he called again, maybe an hour later. Now I was alarmed. "Do you want me to come out there?" I asked.

"No, no," he assured me. "I'm all right. I just needed to ask you something."

"Of course," I replied. "Anything."

"You remember that distinction you made in *Lies My Teacher Told Me*, about two kinds of dead people, from African societies?"

"You mean the *sasha* and the *zamani*," I replied. The beginning of Chapter 10, "Down the Memory Hole," in *Lies My Teacher Told Me*, introduced those terms to many Americans,[1] but they were not my terms. John Mbiti introduced them to me.[2] In brief, "sasha" means "living-dead," ancestors who have died but are still remembered personally by people still alive. In a sense, those in the sasha are not dead, because descendants and acquaintances can bring them back to life by telling anecdotes about them or correcting a sketch artist's attempts to draw them. They may still be remembered this way fifty years after their death.

"Yes, that's it," Gale said. "Well, I want you to promise me that as long as you live, you'll keep me in your sasha." I replied, "That's the easiest thing you could ask of me, Gale. You were like an older brother to me. I'll remember you forever."

Of course, that last word was an exaggeration, but Gale let it pass. He was happy with my reply. Being remembered was important to him. I think it is important to most of us. Certainly Mbiti thinks it's important to Africans: he says the desire to be remembered in the sasha is one reason for people to get married and have children—sometimes more than they can afford.

Today, we have a new form of "immortality"—the internet! While writing this essay, I looked up Gale Brock, a.k.a. Gene Brock (he changed his name), and could not find him on the web.[3] He graduated from the University of Colorado, earned an MA in geography from Oregon, taught at Sacramento State, then started buying homes and apartment buildings, repairing them, and renting them out. At the time of his death, he owned at least fifteen units, I think, and left major bequests to the Sierra Club and other charities. Nevertheless, in Mbiti's words, "Unless a person has close relations to remember him when he has physically died, then he is nobody and simply vanishes out of human existence like a flame when it is extinguished."

One reason I wrote this reflection is to remember Gene, and I shall do so until the moment I join the sasha.

The sasha and zamani resonate with others besides my friend. Kevin Brockmeier quotes my passage on the sasha and zamani as the frontispiece of his novel *The Brief History of the Dead*. Every other chapter then takes place in a weird afterlife, the sasha, an old-fashioned and magical city where people go while someone on earth still remembers them. Nat Hentoff uses the concepts in discussing jazz greats. The distinction seemed useful to me when my mother died; I spoke about it at her memorial service, inviting her grandchildren to remember her and bring her to life as long as they live and whenever they might need her example.

Although the terms are African, Western culture too has rudiments of the distinction between sasha and zamani. Consider the poem "Thanatopsis," meaning contemplation of death, by William Cullen Bryant. It provides a form of comfort to the reader even on the subject of the inevitable passage from sasha to zamani, without ever using the terms:

> . . . what if thou withdraw
> In silence from the living, and no friend
> Take note of thy departure? All that breathe
> Will share thy destiny.[4]

I look forward to the increased use of the terms themselves, however. A side benefit from their employment: few people in our hemisphere have knowingly incorporated intellectual terms from African cultures into their writing and speaking. Doing so helps reduce our ethnocentrism, as we realize that other societies have things to teach us, just as we do them.

The concepts also apply to events. A logical inference is, we know more about recent events, still in the sasha of most Americans, than about distant ones. Simply putting half a dozen people together and asking them what happened at an event they witnessed, even half a century ago, will generate an astonishing amount of detail.[5] This mound of knowledge undermines the all-too-prevalent view that we understand the past better as we get further away from it—the assumption of automatic historical perspective. Yes, recent observers may be more invested in an event. Americans are much more passionate about the War in Vietnam than the War of 1812. Americans born before about 1962 are more passionate about the War in Vietnam than those born later. But that does not necessarily make them more biased. They also know a lot more about it, at least their slice of it.[6]

Historians who write about the more distant past can be even more biased owing to their positions on contemporary issues. A well-known example is the bulk of historical writing in the first half of the twentieth century about Reconstruction. In the age of intense white supremacy known as the Nadir of race relations, 1890–1940, and for two decades thereafter, most historians' racism prevented them from making intelligent use of primary sources from the 1870s. So they made many statements that would have been upended as nonsense if uttered during Reconstruction itself, or immediately afterward. "Further Reflections on Lincoln in History" supplies another example of this point.

Historians who insist on the notion that historical perspective requires time are simply under the influence of the notion of automatic progress. "We're smarter than we used to be." That may hold in physics, but not always in history.

Notes

1 My use of the terms led others to write a Wikipedia page, "Sasha and Zamani," years ago.

2 John Mbiti, *African Religions and Philosophy* (Nairobi: Heinemann, 1969), 25–28. He writes "sasa"; I write "sasha" because the professor who taught Kiswahili at Tougaloo College long ago said "sasha."

3 I did find his name among several hundred commentators on an environmental impact statement in California. Also, one "find a person" web service still listed him, "age 80s," not knowing he had died.

4 Another poem, "So Many Different Lengths of Time," by Brian Patten and Pablo Neruda, makes the distinction and is frequently recited at funerals, but the poets are *not* happy about passing into the sasha.

5 Of course, there will be discord and discrepancies. Thoughtful historians or sociologists have to assess critically the words and their speakers, just as they must think critically about more distant written sources. But as I argued earlier ("Oral History Is More Accurate Than Written Sources"), live sasha sources have additional advantages compared to more distant written sources.

6 Judging from the poor treatment of the War in Vietnam in all but one of the textbooks I reviewed for *Lies My Teacher Told Me*, we shall become much more ignorant about that important topic as soon as it passes into the zamani.

Paddling the Boundary Waters, or Getting to Know the Customs

One year while I was living in Vermont, I got involved in a two-day canoe trip with international implications.[1] The cast of characters included two adults: my friend Annemie, who is Austrian but had lived in Vermont longer than I had, and me, and three children: her son Marcel, fourteen, my son Nick, twelve, and my daughter Lucy, ten. We had two cars and two canoes.

Most rivers in northwestern Vermont flow westward from the Green Mountains to Lake Champlain and then north to the St. Lawrence. The Winooski River is the largest of these, emptying into the lake at Burlington. Next north comes the Lamoille, about which more presently. Our project was to canoe the Missisquoi, the farthest north. According to its 2019 description in Wikipedia, the river is canoeable from Mansonville, Quebec, thirteen miles upstream from East Richford, Vermont, where we planned to put in, all the way to Lake Champlain. It forms part of the Northern Forest Canoe Trail, said to be the longest water trail in the nation, whose website claims the Missisquoi offers "paddling as calm and mellow as the cows grazing at its banks." What could possibly go wrong?

We had intended to leave on Saturday by 10:00 a.m., but somehow getting our food, camping gear, and canoes into and onto the cars took much longer. We left maybe at noon. We drove to what Vermonters call the Northeast Kingdom, the relatively wild northeastern quadrant of the state, and

crossed into Canada near Richford. It is hardly a busy crossing, so our two cars constituted the most excitement of the
day for the customs officers on both sides of the border.
Then we drove east and came back into the US just west of
East Richford. This border crossing has the least use of any
international boundary in Vermont, perhaps in America.[2]
Even in 2020, sometimes as few as three cars use it in a day.

We left both canoes and all three children at a park
on the Missisquoi River right in "downtown" East Richford,
which the river bisects. Then Annemie and I drove both
cars back into Canada. Again, we were quite the commotion
going through customs into Canada and then coming back
out again a few miles west. Near Richford we left a car at
our take-out point, got into one car, and drove back through
customs into Canada, drove a few miles east, then back into
the US through customs to our put-in point. Parking the car,
we got into the canoes and shoved off.

We had gone through customs twelve times in all, and
now it was late afternoon. Our total trip length was going
to be something like ten miles, and we were going to camp
out en route, so we were not really behind schedule. As we
started paddling, however, we faced problems; or, rather,
trees. The Missisquoi had plenty of water, but it was not
very wide. Trees had fallen across it perhaps as often as
every hundred yards.

When we got to a tree, the bow paddler had to step out
onto the trunk, then steady the canoe. The stern person
then clambered up the canoe, crawling over the packs, to
the trunk, and then stepped out onto the opposite side.
Then using the canoe to assist balance, the paddlers hauled
it up and over the trunk and down onto the other side. Then
the bow paddler got in, clambered to the bow, steadied the
canoe, and the stern paddler got in, only to repeat the procedure a few minutes later, at the next obstruction. It was
even worse in our canoe, because we had a third person as

ballast in the middle—someone else to balance on the log as we pulled the canoe over.

At length we reached more open country and began to make better time. But then we came to a beautiful meadow with a particularly impressive tree growing upright right in the middle. Annemie, always the artist, wanted to sketch it. "Can we stop here for dinner and camp here tonight?" she entreated. I knew we had not yet gone even halfway, but how can one argue with an artist? We stopped, admired the tree, pitched our tents under it, and fixed dinner.

The next morning we awoke to a steady rain. I finally figured out that my little gas stove would work in our tent, which was slightly larger, so we fixed some kind of breakfast—probably oatmeal and coffee—while waiting for the rain to let up. It didn't. We realized that in the process of rolling up our sleeping bags, striking our tents, and putting everything into our canoes, which themselves would be filling with rainwater during the process, everything we had would get soaked, including us. We found the prospect grim.

At this point Marcel had a brilliant idea. He pointed out that right across the river was a farmer's meadow, going up a hill to a house, which had a garage, so obviously it was on a road. We could pull our canoes up the meadow, hitchhike down the road back to our put-in vehicle, and abort our trip.

A cloud lifted! Not the rain cloud. Rain continued steadily. But Marcel's words solved the problem! For the first time in my life, I realized that not every trip has to be completed.

We packed up, paddled 40 feet across the river, and unpacked on the other side. Then we pulled the canoes over long wet grass up the hill and knocked on the farmer's door. He answered. "How far are we from East Richford?" we asked.

He looked at me as if I were out of my mind. "This *is* East Richford!" he replied. And indeed it was. We had paddled perhaps three miles, but it was a squiggly river and made a big loop, and we were in fact less than a twenty-minute walk from our put-in point!

We left the kids with the canoes. Annemie and I walked to the car and drove back to our canoes. We put one canoe on the car and all five of us in it, since it was still raining. We trusted Vermonters not to steal the other canoe from the farmer's front yard. Then we set off to fetch the take-out car.

This required going through customs again into Canada, driving west, and going through customs again into the US. When we reached the take-out point, Annemie and Marcel let us off. Then they drove off to Burlington and beyond, to their home in Charlotte. Meanwhile, my children and I drove through customs again into Canada, then drove back east a last time, going through customs into the US once more, and picked up our canoe where we had left it.

We then drove through customs into Canada again, continued west, and went through customs yet again to enter the US. By now the customs officials were beyond laughing, which they had been doing—they just waved us through wordlessly.

We had gone through customs a total of 24 times in two days, canoed for parts of two days, and wound up less than a mile from where we started! Once again, we could have traversed this distance much faster with no canoes, had we simply walked. In fact, we *did* do exactly that on Sunday morning, from the farmer's home to our put-in car.

One conclusion we can draw from this escapade: if terrorists want to cause death and destruction along our northern border, all they have to do is put a canoe on their car and drive through customs ten times. Then they can load it up with anything they want—terrorists, explosives, even (shudder) pot.

Perhaps there is a further lesson to be learned. My grandchildren can read this saga, ages hence, when they as adults do something stupid, and they may feel consoled. They will hear the voice of their grandfather, saying, "You call that stupid? How about *this*? When I was your age, I went through customs a total of 24 times in two days, canoed for the better part of two days, and wound up less than a mile from where I started!" They will feel better.

So may *you*, when you do something stupid.

Notes

1   The title of this chapter is itself a joke: the famed "boundary waters" lie in northern Minnesota and Ontario, Canada. Also called the Quetico-Superior wilderness, it is the largest canoeing area in the world and the home of Region 12 Explorer Scout Canoe Base, which still exists, renamed the Charles L. Sommers Canoe Base.

2   See "Pinnacle Road–East Pinnacle Border Crossing," https://en. wikipedia.org/wiki/Pinnacle_Road%E2%80%93East_Pinnacle_ Border_Crossing.

Further Reflections on the Canadian Boundary

Our national boundary with Canada has often been called "the longest unfortified border in the world." It has to be, because it's the longest border in the world. Hopefully it will never be fortified, because a wall would wreak havoc on wildlife for more than 3,000 miles.

Furthermore, as we proved with our little canoe caravan, even at those sites where officialdom does hold sway, the border is porous to things, substances, and even people. The solution to making borders "work" is sociological, not physical. And it was working fine when Annemie and I tested it.

The American colonies and later the United States kept trying to take Canada, as late as the War of 1812. I suggest that all Americans should be glad that we didn't. At several points in our history, the existence of Canada has proven invaluable to the United States. After the Revolutionary War, thousands of Loyalists relocated to Canada to escape the ire of their neighbors. Many African Americans had enlisted with the British army or navy, because Great Britain offered them freedom. As the British left, defeated, some of their black allies left with them and relocated, particularly to Nova Scotia.

Canada played a major role in the two biggest periods of lawless behavior in the United States, the 1850s and the 1920s—the kidnapping era and Prohibition. The Fugitive Slave Act, part of the Compromise of 1850, was the most draconian law passed before the Civil War. Under it, a white Southerner could claim that an African American was their slave, even in Northern states like Pennsylvania or Massachusetts. That triggered a hearing before a federal magistrate, not a state court, which might be unreliable in its zeal to enforce slave recapture. In this federal court, blacks could not testify against whites, so prisoners had no voice, unless they were lucky enough to have a good white friend who knew of the proceeding and showed up as a witness. Moreover, the judge got paid $375 in today's terms if he found for the prisoner and $750 if he found for the white claimant, so a bribe was built right into the law.

As a result, even free blacks who had never lived in the South or never been enslaved at all now found themselves in great peril. The book and movie *Twelve Years a Slave* tell how Solomon Northup got kidnapped into slavery while living in upper New York State. A chapter in my book *Lies Across America* tells of the extent of this criminal trade in Delaware and Maryland. African Americans' only safe course was to move to Canada, and many did, including Josiah Henson, famous as the model for "Uncle Tom" in *Uncle Tom's Cabin*. In Ontario, they founded small black towns and also settled in interracial towns. When the Civil War happened, and especially when the 13th Amendment ended slavery, many moved back to the United States, but some of the black neighborhoods remain.

Without Canada, what would they have done?

Canada's existence gave me great peace of mind in 1967. At that point, I had concluded that our war in Vietnam was neither humane nor in our country's realpolitik best interest. At that time, I was in graduate school in sociology at Harvard. Many students at Harvard had come to similar conclusions. Since they had the means, they took out ads in the *New York Times* and the *Harvard Crimson* proclaiming "Hell No! We Won't Go!" This was a good way to make an impact, if one had the money to pay one's share of the ads. The *Crimson* then wrote a first-rate news article about the movement. They quoted several students who had only signed on for the *Crimson* ad and others who had only signed on for the *Times*. Money was not the issue. Rather, some students explained that they had to keep their opposition to the war secret from their parents, lest they stop paying their tuition, so they couldn't let their names appear in the *Times*. This struck me as hypocritical: one could never persuade one's friends, teachers, the people one knew and perhaps had influenced, to be antiwar because they would never know. What kind of antiwar statement was that? Others were happy to let their home communities know of their stance but had to keep it quiet at Harvard, because they were in ROTC (the Reserve Officers' Training Corps). Their hypocrisy was of an even higher order: they *were* going to go, and they knew it; they just wanted the prestige antiwar protesters enjoyed.

Unsatisfied with this approach, I wrote a letter to my own draft board. I began, "Over the course of the past two years it has become clear that the present military activity of the United States in Vietnam is not in the best interest of the United States or of Vietnam." I still hold to that conclusion today. I went on to say that "the moral duty of any conscientious citizen becomes clear. He must oppose the waging of this war with his whole influence."[1] I concluded, "Therefore, I herewith transmit to you my refusal to accept military service, should I be inducted, while the United States is engaged in its military enterprise in Vietnam."

Deliberately, I sent a copy to my hometown newspaper. I invited a story, because these were the people—my school friends, neighbors, Scout leaders—who knew me best. If I could influence anyone, it would be them.

Nothing happened at first. Then the *Decatur Herald* published a huge story on me. They had interviewed at least ten people who knew me and asked their opinion of my stance. Mine was the first antiwar statement in Decatur, and they published it to coincide with the progress of a "peace torch" through the city, on a coast-to-coast journey across the nation.

I had no idea what would happen to me. I hoped nothing would, of course. But Canada as an escape hatch was definitely a possibility. I did not want to go to jail and had no illusion that I might get "easy time."

I learned later that at least one of the five members of my local draft board was furious with my letter. He raised the question, "What can we do to him?" But the army didn't want my ilk; it was already struggling with many soldiers and sailors who were against the war. Luckily for me the attorney for the Selective Service Board said they should do nothing, lest I raise the issue of free speech. Both of these men happened to live on my block, in a city of 70,000! In the end, they did nothing to me. But Canada did provide an escape hatch for thousands of my peers, who were not so lucky.

Canada also provides interesting examples of how to do things differently. Health care is the most prominent example. Canada spent about 10.5% of its GDP on health care, while we spent more than 17%, according to World Bank statistics for 2016. Yet Canadians enjoy lifespans of 82 years, while Americans only live to 78.6 years, on average.[2]

The more Americans learn about Canada, perhaps the less ethnocentric we shall become. I regret that visiting Canada now requires a passport. That can only decrease the number of Americans who visit and learn from our northern neighbor. Moreover, imagine how long our 24 border crossings would have taken had we been forced to show passports each time.

Notes

1   Yes, I wrote "he." Everyone did, back then. Besides, only males *were* required to register for the military draft then. Interestingly, today

we have fixed the sexism of the language, but not the Selective Service.

2 Selena Gonzales, Marco Ramirez, and Bradley Sawyer, "How Does U.S. Life Expectancy Compare to Other Countries?," Kaiser Family Foundation, April 4, 2019, https://www.healthsystemtracker.org/chart-collection/u-s-life-expectancy-compare-countries/#item-start.

The Strainer

One river near Vermont has plenty of white water all summer long, because it is a dam release. Unlike the Missisquoi, it is also broad, so there is no chance that trees might fall across it. This is the last section of the Sacandaga River, in New York State. It flows from a reservoir created by Stewart's dam, about three miles east to the Hudson River.

It is a big tourist destination, in a low-key Northwoods way. The Town of Hadley runs a shuttle bus for a dollar, taking inner-tubers up to the top of the run so they can float down. One summer John Duell, with whom I had taken my abortive trip down the Sangamon River three decades earlier, visited me in Burlington, Vermont, with his wife Trish and two teenage daughters, all the way from London, where John was now an architect. Wanting to show them a good time, something they could talk about in England for years, I suggested we tube the Sacandaga. Not knowing what they were getting into, they agreed.

John helped me put my canoe on my little Toyota Tercel hatchback. Then I jammed big inflated truck inner tubes onto the stern of the canoe. The car looked bizarre but I was able to drive it. The wind resistance must have been astonishing.

We drove down the night before and camped out on Great Sacandaga Lake. John took his family out on the lake in my canoe and was terribly proud he could still do it: "Once a Canoe Baser always a Canoe Baser," he said, and he had every right to brag, since it had been more than 30 years since he had even been in a canoe.

The next day, it was time for the Sacandaga. The first part of the run is a long series of Class II rapids caused by a "rock garden," a series of rocks and small boulders, mostly just under the surface, and I did think to tell my crew about the critical command "bottoms up!" It means, as you are lolling back on your inner tube, stomach to the sky, pull up your backside so it does not hit the rocks that may lurk only a few inches below the surface. I also taught them how to go left and right on the flowing river by "ferrying"—swimming upstream at an angle.

But I did not teach them to avoid strainers. A strainer is a tree that has fallen into the river, usually perpendicular to the bank, creating a hazard part of the way across. The water pressure of a river flowing through a partly submerged tree can pin a paddler or a tuber against its branches with surprising force. A tuber wearing a life jacket lost her life when trapped against this strainer in Pennsylvania.

But I had never heard of a strainer on the Sacandaga and never encountered one on any prior float. What could possibly go wrong?

I was paddling my aluminum canoe solo. The trip was more fun in an inner tube, and probably easier too, but I wanted to see if I could canoe it competently.

The middle part of the river was simply a fast-flowing stream, fun to go down on a tube, and fun also in a canoe. At the end, the Sacandaga narrowed to become a Class III flume, but still not much navigation was required. Any rocks were several feet down; the rush of water created waves but should not sink my canoe with only one person in it.

I would bring up the rear, to ensure that none of my four guests lagged behind or had a problem. On canoe trips this person is called "the sweep."

Of course, we came upon a strainer. A tree had fallen into the river from the right bank. It only covered a third of the broad stream, but I could see people getting hung up on its branches. To my horror, one of those was my guest, Trish Duell. I watched helplessly from well upstream as she and her inner tube went through and under! I still don't understand how the inner tube could come out the other side, but come out it did, and Trish too, unscathed.

Not so unscathed was a twelve-year-old girl. Her father had tied a small rope to her inner tube and tied the other end around her wrist, so she would not become separated from it. Now she was holding on to a limb, trying to stay safely above the water, while her inner tube was getting sucked under the tree. The rope pulled and chafed her arm.

Her father had a knife and was trying to clamber out onto the tree to his daughter but was finding it tough going. I picked him up and used all my strength to back up against the current and then delivered him to his daughter. He cut the rope, and both of them made their way across the strainer to shore.

The flume provided its usual rush, and although I had remembered to tell the Duells to stay right and get to the right bank when the Sacandaga hit the Hudson, I again watched from the rear as first Trish and then their daughter Emily went too far and nearly wound up going across the broad Hudson River. My own daughter Lucy had once done this, when she was even younger than Emily, and I had to get in my car and drive over a bridge to retrieve her from the east bank, but she was not hurt or even really worried.

Trish and Emily *were* worried, but they did the right thing: they swam really hard, using the inefficient backstroke that lying in an inner tube imposes. Exhausted, eventually they reached the west bank of the Hudson, where the rest of us were waiting for them.

"We were shattered but able to retell the tale many times," Trish told me, years later. So, you see, they *did* talk about it in England for years. Hence, I submit, really, *nothing* went wrong!

Capsizing on Flat Water

My Grumman aluminum canoe, which I had bought at Canoe Base, had served me well in Vermont, even though it really wasn't a good river canoe. For one thing, it had a keel. Even if only about three-fourths of an inch high, this helped a paddler keep the boat going straight on a lake, especially with a cross wind, but only made it harder to maneuver on a river. Also, aluminum is sticky. It seems to have an affinity for rocks, and when you hang up on a shallow underwater rock in an aluminum canoe, you almost have to lift the canoe off. It doesn't want to slide. By now my canoe had left shiny traces of itself on river rocks all over northern Vermont.

It also was heavy, weighing in at 80 pounds including glued-in kneeling pads and a big flotation bag in the center. But it worked . . . and I'm cheap.

Then someone stole it, right from my back yard!

Now I had to get a new canoe. I don't remember why I decided to get a C1. A C1 is much shorter, made of plastic, and comes with a spray skirt, like a kayak. It seats one person. You have probably seen one on a river but thought it was a kayak. The defining difference is, you sit in a kayak. In a C1, you kneel. Also, C1 paddles look like canoe paddles, so they have only one blade. Kayak paddles of course have blades on both ends and are rarely made of beautiful wood, like canoe paddles often are.

For some reason, I defined myself as a canoeist, not just

a paddler. I don't know why, but somehow I thought canoes were better. Of course, I had never had much experience in a kayak.

Anyway, the main canoe store in northern Vermont had a beautiful little red C1, and I bought it, along with a paddle and spray skirt. Made of a rubberized material, the spray skirt clamps around your midsection like a girdle, once you step into it and pull it up. Then you walk around the woods with it on you, like a tutu. Around the outside is a bungee cord, sewn into a hem. When your C1 is on the water ready to go, you step into it and kneel on the bottom. Then you use river water to wet the lip that goes around the opening. That lubricates the bungee hem, which you now stretch over the lip in all directions. Sometimes a new skirt is so tight that it takes two people to stretch it over this lip. The skirt winds up so taut that you can bounce a quarter on it.

At the front of the skirt is a "grab loop," a plastic rope or tape that you grasp to pull the spray skirt off the craft. Before setting forth, you must practice pulling this loop. If you cannot dislodge the skirt, you might not be able to get out of the boat, even if upside down.

The canoe came with a lesson. Zack, the guy who had sold it to me, would give me pointers on a real river, in real rapids. First, he would teach me how to roll.

We were paddling the section of the Lamoille River that I knew better than any other, the five-mile run from Fairfax to Arrowhead Mountain Lake. Zack was experienced; indeed, he also served as an officer in the Northern Vermont Canoe Cruisers, the club I belonged to. What could possibly go wrong?

We put in where Vermont 104 crosses the river, the usual put-in spot. I wore a helmet, which I never did on the Lamoille in my regular canoe. C1s are notoriously tippy, so I might spend part of my time on the river upside-down. Although the canoe store tried to sell me a helmet especially made for paddling, I made do with my bicycle helmet, strapped securely under my chin. Seemed to me if it worked for a curb on a street it would work for a boulder in a river.

Zack helped me get in the boat and hook my spray skirt onto the canoe. It worked fine; I could pull it off without a problem.

Right at the start came the first rapid, a Class II that required going through a chute at the left bank, then cutting sharply right to find deeper water in the center of the stream. I had done it many times without incident in my regular two-person open canoe ("OC-2"), even with new bow paddlers who had never been in a canoe before. This time I entered the chute just fine, turned right, and immediately tipped over.

I must explain that although a C1 looks like a kayak, tipping over in one is a bigger deal. Because you kneel in a canoe, even though your legs are bent double on the bottom of the boat, you still ride much higher than when you sit on the bottom of a kayak. Therefore your center of gravity is higher. As a result, completing a "roll," the maneuver to bring you back on top of the river again, is much harder.

I tried but didn't know what I was doing. Rather than stay upside down and drown, I made a "wet exit": I pulled the grab loop, straightened my knees, and pushed out of my C1, holding on to it. Then I floundered to the shore to get in again.

In a quiet eddy in the stream, Zack got out of his C1, stood in the waist-deep water, and helped me practice rolling. After tilting my canoe into the water, or having me do so simply by leaning, he then taught me to lean forward, put my canoe paddle on the surface of the water above me, paddle down hard, forcing my head and body above the water, and get a good breath of air. I felt better: I didn't have to exit the boat fast enough to breathe; I could get my head above water while still in it.

Then I was to do the same thing again, only more strongly, swiveling my hips under me, thus righting the craft with me in it.

I couldn't do it. I asked Zack to do it, to show me. He did, but only about a third of the time, and that was in flat water.

I tried some more. I still couldn't do it. Years later, in Washington, DC, I took a kayaking class and did learn to roll a kayak, although not consistently. But I never rolled my C1. Not once.

There seemed nothing to do but set forth again, down the Lamoille. Soon we were in the "rock garden," a series of small boulders that required maneuvering around, finding "downstream V's" in the river between them. In my old canoe, I had usually left shiny shards of aluminum on various rocks in this section. My C1 was far more maneuverable, being so much shorter and with no keel, so I was able to go exactly where I intended, getting through without incident. When I did scrape a rock, the C1 seemed to bounce off it, whereas my old canoe would have stuck to it.

I did turn over two more times, however, and each time I had to make a wet exit. I couldn't even manage to right myself by putting my paddle vertical and pushing against the bottom of the stream, a maneuver that is somewhat questionable in the first place, since the paddle can jam between rocks and break or get separated from its owner. Zack enjoyed the humor of my predicament, but I was disturbed that I could not get down a Class II rapid that I could always paddle in my old metal boat.[1]

Finally we got though the rock garden. Now we were paddling in flowing but nearly flat water, dammed up by Five Chutes, the last rapid on the river before our take-out at Arrowhead Mountain Lake. To my astonishment, I tipped over one last time above Five Chutes. One moment I was paddling along, not paying much attention to the water, just enjoying the scenery. The next, my canoe had tilted quickly to the left. I was paddling on the right, and although I could have done a "high brace"—paddle upright in the water, leaning far to the right, then pulling hard to keep from flipping left, I wasn't quick enough.

Once more I made a wet exit. "What was *that*?" I sputtered at Zack, having once more reached the bank. He was enjoying my comic distress. "That was flat water!"

"Look carefully," Zack replied. "See the eddy line?"

And there it was, an almost invisible line between the main body of the Lamoille, moving downstream at maybe 2 mph, and an area of flat water nearer the bank, moving upstream at perhaps ½ or ¼ mph. I hadn't paid attention and had drifted sideways from downstream to upstream. Immediately my C1 had flipped. Five Chutes is a series of low, flat rocks across the Lamoille, sticking out of the river maybe two feet, dividing it into five little streams. In August, only one of those chutes was usually runnable. Since it required some maneuvering, canoe clubs gave Five Chutes a Class III ranking, although it was an easy III.[2]

I took grave care through Five Chutes. Basically, I went through it in a low brace position, not paddling at all, leaning left, paddle held flat at the water's surface on the left side, ready to counterbalance whatever forces threatened to flip me. I felt like I was riding a unicycle on greased linoleum, and I realized I would *never* get good enough at paddling a C1 to enjoy it.

We took out at the lake a little below Five Chutes. As I unbent my legs and stood up, they ached. My knees hurt. Zack explained that even Olympic C1 paddlers look like elderly duffers when they try to stand up at the end of a run. "Why am I doing this to myself?" I asked myself again. A C1 was doubtless a great craft for a great canoeist. It was a terrible choice for an average paddler, like me.

I sold the boat back to the store. Zack offered me what I paid for it in trade for a new OC-2. My new two-person boat was everything my old Grumman was not: lighter, keelless, more maneuverable, averse to rocks. I couldn't roll it, but then again, I wouldn't flip it. At least not on the Lamoille. At least not in average conditions.[3]

I was ready for further adventures with a paddle.

Notes

1　The chapter titled "My Paddling Makes the Evening News," starting on p. 119, tells how the rock garden changed in a hundred-year flood, so I must qualify "always."

2　As paddlers have improved, ratings of rapids have gone down. I suspect Five Chutes is now ranked Class II.

3　Again, see the chapter to come titled "My Paddling Makes the Evening News."

The Mad River Lives
Up to Its Name

Mad River has been a good name for the canoe company, and in fact the first Mad River canoe was developed within a mile of the river, in Waitsfield, Vermont. However, it's not really a good canoeing river. In the summer it's usually a creek, too low to be canoed. In spring, it has plenty of water from the melting snow runoff, but then it's too cold to be paddled safely without a drysuit or perhaps a really good wetsuit.

An unusually warm day (for Vermont) in, say, early May offers the best hope for a fun if not safe trip down the river. My then girlfriend Karen responded to such a warm Saturday by suggesting that four of us—she and I along with David, my best male friend, and Gail, a woman he was going out with—make a trip of it.

I did not know what David and Gail knew about canoe-ing or white water. David owned a canoe, and Gail had lived on the Mad River and canoed it before. They both exuded confidence that they knew what they were doing. So I didn't see it as my role to tell them what to do, especially because I had not set up the trip in the first place.

Karen and I had paddled before, so she knew at least the basics. I did remind Karen to be sure that all her belong-ings were tied into the canoe, like mine. Also, I told her to keep her paddle parallel to the water, sticking out from the boat, ready to brace.

We unloaded the two canoes at the put-in point in

Warren. Highway 100 parallels the river as it flows north toward its confluence with the larger Winooski River, which then flows west to Lake Champlain. We planned to paddle through Waitsfield to Moretown, two-thirds of the way to that confluence, maybe a fourteen-mile paddle.

I didn't really think about what might go wrong, since it wasn't really "my" trip. But I should have, anyway. After all, Route 100 parallels the Mad River closely. I might have taken advantage of its proximity to the river and gotten us to stop frequently to ensure that it was all canoeable by people of our modest abilities. But I didn't.

We also never checked the temperature of the water. Even when we got in the canoes, we took care *not* to let our feet get wet, presuming it was cold.

But then, a successful canoe manufacturing company is named for the Mad River. Obviously, it must be canoeable. What could possibly go wrong?

We launched. David and Gail led. The rapids were Class II, not really easy, but we were handling them fine. Karen and I watched them enter the most difficult rapid, a Class III. I shared an early draft of this essay with Karen, and she remembered that rapid as quite foreboding, saying: "Then we heard the sound of a waterfall. . . . It seemed really high to me—eight feet at least." We watched David and Gail tilt suddenly to the right as their canoe hit what is called a "hole," a spot of much lower water just downstream of a submerged rock. Immediately they capsized, and both were "swimming," though the water was just waist high. Or, in Karen's account, "They seemed to go straight down with the bow slamming into the water, bounced out of their seats, tipped the boat when they both came down off center, and lost all their gear. Immersed in snow melt, they desperately headed to the nearby shore, letting everything float away." Rushing water can be treacherous—if you stand up too fast, it can pitch you forward—but they held on to their canoe and paddles and scrambled as fast as they could to get out of the water and onto the bank.

Then Karen and I set forth into the rapid. I learned decades later that this surprised Karen: "Now I thought for sure we would portage around the falls, but you said, 'See, they would have been all right if they had kept their paddles parallel to the water so they could correct for tipping.'"

Despite their example and my alleged expertise, in a few seconds we hit the same hole and capsized to our right exactly as they had done. The water was cold—astonishingly cold. It was snow runoff, and though the air was warm, the water had not had much chance to warm up. I suspect it was in the low 40s. I had never experienced anything like it. We too held on to our canoe and paddles and soon joined David and Gail on the bank, gasping from the cold but enjoying the much warmer air. Karen remembers, "A waterfall can sound like laughter, and I felt like we were the brunt of a joke about underestimating the power of water—especially when it is called a Mad River."

There was a house 50 yards downstream, the residents of which Gail happened to know. She asked them if we might use their dryer, in their carport. Soon all four of us took off all our clothes except our underpants, put everything in the dryer, and stood around making small talk in the near-nude.

This was way back in 1983, so David and I sneaked glances at both women. Maybe they sneaked glances at us. Of course, I feel sure nothing like that would happen today, when everyone is so much more refined. But our canoeing never led to canoodling, at least not in the carport.[1]

What to do next? Karen and I were fired up to finish the trip. David and Gail had had enough. Their morale was shot, partly because they listed five different items that had been in their canoe and were now going down the Mad River. I don't remember how they got back to their car, which we

had left at the put-in point upstream, but I suspect that we had not gone very far. Probably they just walked.

Karen and I relaunched our canoe and paddled the rest of the Mad River without incident. On the way, we recovered four of the five lost items—clothing, even a water bottle—stuck on branches or bobbing in eddies. The only item we never found was David's sweater, which unfortunately was a favorite of his. Nevertheless, I thought we had done rather well. Reaching Karen's van, we put the canoe on top and returned home. Later we got David's and Gail's recovered items back to them.

The Mad River illustrates the problem with several Vermont streams: either they are too cold to paddle (in April and May) or they are too dry (June through September). That quandary was actually one reason for my later relocation to Washington, DC, where the rivers are warmer in spring and deeper in summer. I suppose another useful life lesson was: early in a relationship, you want to suffer a canoeing fiasco.[2] You learn a lot about your paddling partner, more than ever surfaces during a merely pleasant day on the river. In this case, Karen and I found we were well matched, even if our partnership never came to full fruition off the river, and we remain friends to this day, decades later. Other partners I've had, two in particular, I wish I'd vetted via a canoeing mishap. I might have found out something about their character that could have saved me years of heartache.

I suspect they feel the same!

Notes

1   I thought about titling this chapter "Half Naked in a Carport," hoping desperately to sell more books, but gave it up in favor of truth in packaging.
2   Never did I contrive a fiasco. I seem to have had enough just in my normal paddling practice.

Stumped

I claim to be a woodworker. While I have never success-fully completed a dovetail joint, I have managed some beautiful picture frames, three coffee tables, and a round dining table that began life as a Texaco sign. I have also increased the housing stock of the planet by one and two halves houses.

Actually, I am a self-taught carpenter with delusions of grandeur. You can discern a pattern, since I also claim to be a whitewater canoeist.

Probably my most successful woodworking project dates to my formative years at Tougaloo College in Mississippi, after Canoe Base but before Vermont. After living on campus for three years, my wife and I bought a house on Oak Hill Drive in Jackson, the state capital. Unlike most street names, applied solely to boost property values, the street actually did have a hill on it, with a big red oak tree.

Shortly after we moved in, a thunderstorm hit the area, a bolt of lightning hit the oak, and the old tree came down. Its trunk turned out to be mostly hollow, so I bought a chain saw and cut off a four-foot section of it. I then spent the better part of two days with my hatchet, taking off the bark and making the remaining walls thinner and lighter. Eventually I filled the ends with cedar boards, hinged a split part of the trunk to make a lid, and fashioned walnut feet to keep it from rolling. The result, which we call our "trunk trunk," has become a family heirloom.[1]

After moving to Vermont, I was interested in repeating this triumph. Eventually I came upon a likely possibility. I lived in Queen City Park, a majority-French-Canadian neighborhood on beautiful Shelburne Bay, part of Lake Champlain. One day, when driving around the southern end of the bay, I got out of my car and looked around. A small creek flowed into the bay from the south. Over to the right someone had dumped into the bay an enormous stump that they had bush-hogged from their property. Leaving it in the lake was doubtless easier than taking it to the dump, which would have also charged a fee.

I decided to harvest the stump and make something out of it—another coffee table, perhaps. The tree had been cut levelly and flat, in a clean single cut. It was nearly five feet across, so it could sit upside down on a floor, I thought. Then I could use a water level to mark all the big and little roots at exactly the same height, maybe 30 inches, saw them off, and lay a curved piece of thick plate glass on top. These roots curved around and about and formed quite a filigree. Seeing all that through the glass would be beautiful!

First, of course, I had to get it home. Queen City Park lies at the northeast corner of the bay, almost three miles north. I planned to invite someone to join me in this adventure; we would paddle my canoe the length of the bay, tie a rope around the stump, and paddle back. When I reached Queen City Park, since I knew everyone, it would be easy to recruit several neighbors to help lift the stump from the water, carry it up the sloping bank, and wrestle it into the back of my 1949 pickup truck. What could possibly go wrong?

I called Glenda, a woman I knew from church, and she was up for the adventure. She already knew how to paddle, and besides, it was flat water. We would not capsize.

It was a lovely summer afternoon. We paddled the length of the bay in less than an hour, found the stump, and tied it to the canoe. Next we got out of the canoe into the lake, with our feet on the muddy bottom, and wrestled the stump into deeper water until it floated. Then we got back in. Now it was time to make our way back north.

Paddlers don't really generate much force, but because the outer surface of a canoe is so smooth, they can make four miles per hour on a lake. Not us. We paddled and paddled, making almost no progress. According to Wikipedia, a "sea anchor is a device that is streamed from a boat in heavy weather. Its purpose is to stabilize the vessel and to limit progress through the water." Obviously, we were towing a highly effective sea anchor. We were completely stable but getting nowhere. I did the math in my head. An hour of paddling with our anchor had advanced us perhaps half a mile. It was now nearing 4:00 p.m. At this rate, we would reach Queen City Park around 9:30, in complete darkness. No one would be out and about. For that matter, boating in darkness without lights on Lake Champlain, even just in a canoe, was neither prudent nor legal. I shared the math with my bow partner. We needed a new plan.

Just then a boat with outboard motor came past. Its occupants knew Glenda, and she called out to them. They agreed to help us. She threw them the rope from the front of our canoe, they tied it to their boat, and then they turned up the throttle on their motor.

Immediately I realized that I had inadvertently converted my canoe into part of the tow line connecting their power boat to the stump. The strain put my craft in jeopardy. The breastplates, bow and stern, separated from the sides, and the entire boat threatened to come apart. I almost brought this to the attention of our Good Samaritans, but I feared if they let us go, they might not tie us back up again. So I just sat back in the canoe and hoped it would hold together.

Even with a strong outboard motor, our return to Queen

City Park still proved excruciatingly slow. Finally, our little caravan reached the north side of the bay. Our Samaritans untied our line from their boat, we thanked them, and they pulled away. Paddling past the swimming area, we made quite a sight, which was good, because we got the attention of swimmers and sunbathers on Red Rocks Park beach, adjacent to Queen City Park's little shoreline landing area. I walked up the road to my house and got my pickup truck. Meanwhile, Glenda recruited several men, bored from lying in the sun, to help lift.

Five or six of us easily wrangled the stump up the hill to the road and into the back of my pickup truck. I drove to my driveway, backed up next to my shed, and Glenda and I managed to get it out of the truck.

It sat there, next to my shed, for two years. I realized that if I made it 30" high, I would have to cut off most of the interesting roots and rootlets, so it would have to be 36". No one ever had a coffee table three feet high! Even 30" was twice as high as the coffee tables I had built in the past. Moreover, the whole thing would be far too large in diameter for any space I might ever own. It would be a perfect centerpiece for the lobby of an over-the-top hotel or a truly rich law firm's reception area, but I had no idea how to reach out to that market or if it even existed in Vermont. The whole situation stumped me.

Eventually I moved from Vermont and left it there to rot. When last I visited "my house," 25 years later, it was gone.

Later I realized that, like many of my canoeing experiences, the trip was its own reward. It had been an enjoyable afternoon, after all. We had solved interesting problems, one after another. Even my canoe seemed none the worse for the wear; once separated from the strain of pulling the sea anchor, it slipped back into shape, and I used it for years. If the final goal—a beautiful piece of furniture—proved ephemeral, well, maybe the entire sequence was just one more way that canoe trips imitate life itself.

Notes

1   Or at least I hope it will. I'm not dead yet, though I am working on it.

Reflections on Home Buying in Mississippi and Vermont

In 1971, when my then-wife and I went house shopping in Mississippi, it was like buying bell peppers in a supermarket: lots of choices. In one neighborhood alone, two or three houses were for sale on each block. Of course, there was some history behind this convenience, and some race relations. The schools had just desegregated, which in turn led to blockbusting.

The background was, white leaders of Mississippi had spent two centuries telling their constituents that since blacks were inferior, first slavery and later segregation were appropriate for them. Politicians had also spent the sixteen years after the 1954 *Brown* decision mandated school desegregation shouting "Never!" Then, suddenly, in the middle of the school year, on January 5, 1970, more than 40 school districts across the state, including Jackson, desegregated. The change had been scheduled for the start of the 1969–70 school year, but Mississippi's senior senator, John Stennis had worked a deal with President Richard Nixon: as chair of the Armed Forces Committee, he would give Nixon what he wanted to continue the Vietnam War. In turn, Nixon would make the US Departments of Justice and of Health, Education, and Welfare flip sides and argue to delay school desegregation in Mississippi. District Court Judge Harold Cox, notoriously racist, happily agreed. Civil rights attorneys then brought his decision to the US Supreme Court (*Alexander v. Holmes County*), which ordered the delay to

end at the close of the fall semester. It turned out fortui-
tous: whites didn't have time to organize private schools to
circumvent desegregation, so in most districts, black and
white children went to school together for the first time.

Now white Mississippians realized that they were not
all-powerful. If an African American family moved next
door to them, they no longer had the clout to stop them.
Their choices were limited to their own behavior: stay or
move.

Unscrupulous realtors[1] played on these fears: "I can get
you $15,000 for your home now, but after it becomes a black
neighborhood, you'll be lucky to get $12." Whites began
fleeing to the suburbs. In the Northside Drive neighborhood
in particular, "For Sale" signs sprouted everywhere.

Realtors were taken aback when we, a white family,
wanted to see homes in this area. The less classy agents
asked bluntly, "You know that's a nigger neighborhood,
right?"[2] When we said yes, they went ahead and showed us
the homes. More sophisticated realtors put it more vaguely,
"You know about the neighborhood, right?" Again, after we
said yes, they showed us the homes.

That behavior is part of a larger practice commonly
called "steering," which realtors use to channel home
buying by race. Doing so benefits real estate agents directly,
because it causes more sales. At the same time, it makes it
harder for black families to build home equity, because they
are competing with all upwardly mobile black families when
they buy into a newly integrated area, but when they sell,
years later, typically the neighborhood has become mostly
black and is not in particular demand. But there seemed to
be some common sense involved, as well. Agents did not
want to waste clients' time, or their own, showing houses
futilely in areas where they had no intention of living.

White residents in the neighborhood who were not
selling might previously have shunned faculty members

at a black college. Now they welcomed us, realizing that we might help keep the neighborhood from going all-black after all. And indeed, almost 40 years after we bought on Oak Hill Drive, our block is still interracial.

Four years later, after divorcing and moving to Vermont, I experienced similar behavior from realtors in New England. Since I was a college professor, they all thought I "should" live in an upper-middle-class neighborhood, replete with IBM managers, doctors, lawyers, and other college professors, preferably in suburban Essex Junction.

When I asked to see houses in the Old North End in Burlington or Queen City Park in South Burlington, they said, "You know about the neighborhood, right?" Again, after I said yes, they showed us—my five-year-old son and me—the homes. This time, what they wanted me to "know about the neighborhood" was not that African Americans were moving in, but rather that it was majority French Canadian.[3]

In my first month in Vermont, I heard every stereotypical adjective I'd ever heard applied to African Americans in Mississippi applied to French Canadian Americans. They were lazy, stupid, irresponsible, criminal, and also bad in bed. (That last was a shocker. Whites never accused blacks of bad bed performance, and I had thought that the French were known to be adroit lovers too. Apparently not *these* French.)

I wound up buying a tiny house in Queen City Park, a cul-de-sac on the "wrong side of the tracks" that was mostly French. Only in Vermont, I thought to myself, would the wrong side of the tracks include the shore of Shelburne Bay, part of beautiful Lake Champlain! The neighborhood seemed amazing to me. It contained 84 units—mostly freestanding homes, but a few triplexes made from larger houses. Everyone knew everyone else, not only because it was a cul-de-sac, but also because we owned some things in common: a tiny fire station (with no truck), our water system, a playground ("the park"), and the lake frontage. I knew my kids, ages four and five, would immediately make friends even if they only wound up living with me during the summers.

It was, however, my first experience living in a stigmatized neighborhood. (The Northside Drive neighborhood in Mississippi was *becoming* stigmatized, although our arrival, and that of other white liberals, slowed the process for a time.) The stigma was brought home to me—indeed, literally upside my head, when, shortly after I moved in, I had a dental appointment. Knowing I was new to Vermont, the dental hygienist asked me where I had chosen to live.

"Queen City Park," I replied.

"How *is* it down there?" she asked, in a tone that implied the further query, "Have you been mugged, raped, or murdered *yet*?" She next said, "Open," and proceeded to do things in my mouth that kept me from speaking further. Then she told me about "the Girards," one of QCP's two dysfunctional families. They lived four doors down from us, in a family unit that now consisted of a grandmother and two or three grandsons in their late teens or early twenties. Their mother was in jail for killing their father, and the boys were said to be out of control.

Incidentally, they never posed a bit of trouble to me or even to their next-door neighbors. On more than one occasion the boys helped my children fix their bicycles. Nevertheless, because it was a "French neighborhood," their notoriety had rubbed off on all the other neighbors, "proving" that nothing good happened among French Canadians.

Realtors despaired of the place. "If only I could bring in clients from the other end!" one said to me at a party, a year after I had moved in. "Then they wouldn't have to see those shacks on Central Avenue." Because I lived in one of "those shacks," I just responded meekly, "I like the neighborhood."

What the South Burlington Public Schools did to neighborhood kids was not amusing, however. My son Nick quickly made friends with "Daniel," three years older. He was the younger child of QCP's other dysfunctional family, and after hearing the shouting that went on among family members, Nick never set foot in Daniel's house again. Nevertheless, I found Daniel to be intelligent and fun. But he couldn't read—he couldn't even figure out "circus" when printed at the bottom of a circus poster. Since Daniel was in third grade, I thought this failure would constitute an educational emergency and he would get extra help. On the contrary: owing to where he lived, his teachers *expected* Daniel to be stupid and rowdy. By seventh grade, he had *become* stupid and rowdy, although he was never rowdy with me, or even stupid, for that matter.

My daughter Lucy soon made friends with "Louise," four doors up the street. Her parents had only graduated from high school. As their relationship grew, Lucy told me that she thought Louise was smarter than she herself was. Nevertheless, college was never an option. Her parents were working-class, and the school system never suggested it; talent from QCP was invisible to teachers. *My* kids escaped this stigma. They might be *in* Queen City Park but they were not *of* Queen City Park. Everyone knew from my attendance at PTA meetings that I was a professor at the University of Vermont with a PhD. As well, Nick and Lucy gave off subtle signals of their social class origins.

Across America, stereotyping neighborhoods has intensified. In some areas, realtors even supply would-be purchasers with average SAT scores for neighborhoods, so "aptitude," which the SAT no longer even claims to measure, becomes another amenity for the upper-middle class home buyers, like a bike path. They know that the right neighborhood, unlike Northside Drive in Mississippi or Queen City Park in Vermont, means that others will accord them status, and teachers will treat their children well. This mind-set punishes diversity, because nonwhites (excepting Asians, to be sure) or working-class whites might lower "standardized test" scores, thereby hurting property values.

The ultimate expression of all this isolation and unequal opportunity by residential area has been the creation of elite sundown suburbs like Edina, near Minneapolis; Kenilworth, on Lake Michigan north of Chicago; and Darien, in Connecticut northeast of New York City. These places have not only kept out African Americans,[4] they also discourage maids, carpenters, firefighters, and even teachers from living within their city limits. One result is that children of the elite grow up within a cocoon in which everyone is rich, white, and college educated, not counting those unfortunate souls who come in from outside to service "us." And those outsiders don't count, not really.

One little change readers can make: when meeting someone who lives in an elite white suburb, don't confer status upon them. After learning where they live, instead of responding, "Oh, it's *beautiful* there, isn't it?" say, "Oh *dear*. Do you have kids?" If they say yes, reply, "And you're raising them in that environment? How sad!" And when buying your home—in Mississippi, Vermont, or anywhere else—make sure to choose a neighborhood that is diverse racially, in social class, and even in age.

Notes

1   I realize that "Realtor," capitalized, denotes a member of the National Association of Realtors. I use the term uncapitalized as a synonym for "real estate agent"; I think most Americans do.

2   Those are exactly the words they used. I wrote this passage in 2019, when using the N-word was controversial. I am not "using" the N-word. I am quoting someone else who used it. White realtors did not say, "You know that's an N-word neighborhood, right?" People deserve to be quoted. Similarly, I am proud that the textbook I wrote on Mississippi history, with coauthors, included a photo of a lynching way back in 1974. Even in 2019, almost no

high school history textbook includes such a photo. Racism is unpleasant and deserves to be shown in all its ugliness.

3   At the time, only 300 African Americans lived in Vermont, and their median household income was at least $2,500 *more* than the median white income. Many had been transferred to Vermont by their employers, including the federal government and armed forces, and had advanced educational degrees. In the absence of poor blacks, however, white Vermonters still proved capable of maintaining racial prejudice. In my first month in Vermont, I heard the N-word more often than I recalled in any month in Mississippi. I even learned it could be a verb: to "nigger" something into place or to "nigger-rig" a home repair meant to do the job badly, so it would shortly fail. This from people who had never had a conversation with an African American!

4   In recent years Edina has taken steps to move beyond its sundown past.

My Paddling Makes
the Evening News

My last summer in Vermont, the Lamoille River experienced extraordinary rain for two straight days in early August. In Burlington, where I lived, it rained, but in the Lamoille watershed it poured, especially on the western slopes of the Green Mountains, where the river begins.

As a result, the Lamoille had a "hundred-year flood," according to the television news. That is a technical term, actually a statistical term, which does not mean that the river will flood like that every hundred years. It does signify a whole lot of water, though. Part of Hardwick, a village of 2,500 people on the Lamoille, was inundated.

Two days later, the crest reached my favorite stretch of the Lamoille, the five-mile run from Fairfax to Arrowhead Mountain Lake—the same stretch that hosted my ill-fated C1 run. It's not only my favorite, it's everybody's: LamoilleRiverPaddlersTrail.org says, "This is a great open boat run for paddlers looking for easy-moderate whitewater suitable for open boats in a beautiful valley away from busy roads." While some Vermonters had experienced economic loss, I saw opportunity: I had never paddled a hundred-year flood before. This was my chance!

I recruited Olivia, my new girlfriend, and she was up for the adventure, since she had not read this book and did not know the breadth and frequency of my canoeing misadventures. My car was a convertible, so we put my canoe atop her car. Then we mounted our two bikes on a rack on the back. We drove to the bridge just above Arrowhead Mountain Lake, just below the most difficult rapids on the entire run, "Five Chutes."

Usually Five Chutes is a series of low flat rocks across the Lamoille, sticking out of the river maybe two feet, dividing it into five little streams. In August, only one of those chutes was usually runnable. Since it required some maneuvering, canoe clubs gave Five Chutes a Class III ranking, although it was an easy III.

This day Five Chutes looked trouble-free. The high water covered all the rocks to a depth of several feet. No chutes were visible. All that remained of the rapids was a standing wave, crossing the river from bank to bank, involving perhaps a one-foot drop. The volume of water was awesome. Nevertheless, I felt reassured. We could certainly handle a one-foot drop. The flood had gentled Five Chutes into a Class I rapid.

Then we drove along Vermont 104A, which parallels the Lamoille on its northern side. About a mile upstream, we stopped to catch a distant glimpse of the "rock garden," the series of rocks and small boulders that, most Augusts, requires some maneuvering to get through without scraping. We couldn't see it well from the road, but as I had expected, the rocks had disappeared. We saw a lot of white spray—the tops of haystacks, interesting water formations that arise when waves from left and right intersect, forming a standing whitecap. These looked to be two feet tall and posed a danger to our open canoe, whose gunwales were less than eight inches above the waterline. But I thought we might successfully pick our way around the larger ones and escape unswamped. I was also reassured to see that everywhere the Lamoille was within its banks. We would not have to contend with the hazard of being pushed among trees or even into strainers.

We drove on to our put-in, where Vermont 104 crosses

the river. Here was the third rapid on our stretch of the river. It was usually a Class II that required going through a chute at the left bank, then cutting sharply right to find deep enough water. But like Five Chutes, the rocks that created this rapid were now far underwater, so it too had become a Class I.

We had now scouted all three of the major hazards on our run. They all looked doable. Besides, it was a sunny day in August. The temperature was in the high 80s. Our run ended in the flat water of a lake. What could possibly go wrong?

My usual procedure when canoeing the Lamoille with just one car was to leave the bikes at the take-out point, locked to a tree. Then we would leave the car at the put-in, paddle down to the take-out, lock the canoe to a tree, and bike back up the road to the car. The technical term for this is "paddle-pedal." Since we usually had to pee after finishing the downstream run, we sometimes called it a "paddle-piddle-pedal."

This time, however, as a precaution, we took an extra step: we left the canoe at the put-in, locked to a tree, then drove the car down to the take-out. Then we biked back up to the canoe and locked our bikes to a tree. That way, if anything did go wrong, we would have a vehicle at our disposal at the bottom.

Everything loose we tied onto the canoe, except our spare paddle. Of course, we were wearing tennis shoes that couldn't slip off and good-quality life jackets. I reviewed with Olivia what to do if we capsized: hold on to the canoe and to the paddle, if you can, but stay upstream of the canoe. A swamped canoe weighs hundreds of pounds and can crush a paddler caught by a rock downstream of it. Swim on your back, with your feet aimed downstream, aiming for the nearest bank. Don't stand up in fast-rushing water; you can get knocked over, break a limb, and even drown. We seemed ready.

Nevertheless, as soon as we launched, I knew we were literally over our heads. I had never paddled a river this powerful before, at least not in an open canoe. (The Colorado through the Grand Canyon was much stronger, but we took that river in six-person rubber rafts with professional guides.) The banks flew by at a dizzying rate. I was totally absorbed in keeping us safe, oriented correctly, and dry. I estimated the banks were going past at more than eight miles per hour, four times the Lamoille's usual speed.

After maybe a mile, I needed to take a break. Usually we would simply aim over to the shore and the bow paddler would find something—a vine, a tree branch, a bull rush—to hold on to. Then the canoe would gently turn around to point upstream, and we could have a drink or just relax for a few minutes. Today, however, I wasn't sure Olivia could hold us against the pressure of this river flow. Nor did I want our canoe to be broadside to the flow, even on purpose, even for a moment.

So I guided us over to the right bank while the river made a gentle right turn. Most of its force would be pressing on the left bank. I asked Olivia to backpaddle while I reached over and grabbed a handful of rushes.

Although I tried to use my arm as a shock absorber, the force of the water pulled the rushes right out of the bank. I grabbed a slim hanging tree limb, and that worked better. Holding the canoe stationary against the current took a toll on my arm and hand, however. A relaxing break this was not. Going with the flow was easier.

In no time, we floated down to the rock garden, now a field of haystacks. We did our best to avoid the larger ones—I would yell "Go right!" and Olivia knew to do a draw stroke. "Go left" meant she did a bow sweep. I was frantically making complementary efforts in the stern. We were doing all right, staying dry—it was more exhilarating than scary.

Looking for haystacks, I never really saw the hole. Suddenly, just to Olivia's left, there was no water. Well, there was, but three feet below the rest of the river. It had poured over some rock, deep below the surface, and mostly gone off to the right and left, I guess. Anyway, our canoe did what objects will do when unsupported on one side: it tilted left and literally fell into the hole.

We too fell out and to the left, of course, but we both remembered to hold on to the boat, which was now below us and to our right, and to hold on to our paddles. We lay on our backs, heads upstream, trying to kick toward the left bank. Our view downstream was completely blocked by the upside-down canoe that we held on to with our left hands. So we had no way to prepare for what was to come.

Suddenly a giant yank wrenched the canoe from our hands. We both lost our grips on our paddles, too. Alarmed, I lay on my back, aimed upstream and to my left, and swam as hard as I could for the left bank. As I did, I saw Olivia closer to the center of the river, moving upstream! I knew she was in a recirculating hydraulic, created when the water flows down into a hole so quickly that it then curves back upstream at the bottom. The Lamoille had never had a recirculating hydraulic before, and I hoped I had told Olivia to swim out the bottom, which is what you're supposed to do. She disappeared from my view upstream.

At last, gasping for air from swimming so hard, I reached shallow water at the left bank and stood up to look around. Olivia was already standing upstream—the hydraulic had spit her out toward the shore. "I'm *so sorry*, Olivia," I said, ashamed of the peril that I had put her in. She shrugged it off—apparently her journey was scarier to witness than to experience. I did notice, however, that she never really wanted to go whitewater canoeing again with me.

Downstream, we couldn't see anything we owned—no trace of our paddles or even my canoe. Nor was there a road on the south bank of the river. When we clambered up to dry land, we found ourselves in a huge field of wild raspberries, which did not provide a sweet ending to our tale. On the contrary, they proved yet another obstacle, since we had to pick our way between the bushes carefully, lest their prickers scratch our bare legs. Olivia had to walk behind me, because the force of the hydraulic had sucked out both her contact lenses. She couldn't see where she was going without me in front.

Eventually, we made our way to a gravel road and walked toward the west. It would have to hit the road that crossed the river at Five Chutes, I thought. I hoped at least the canoe and maybe even a paddle or two would be visible when we got to Arrowhead Mountain Lake. But we had walked barely half a mile when a pickup truck came along behind us. We raised thumbs to flag a ride. The driver stopped.

"You're the ones we're looking for!" he said to us. It turned out that the Volunteer Fire and Rescue Squads of Georgia and Milton Vermont were holding training exercises that afternoon at the parking lot where the Lamoille entered the lake. They had seen my canoe floating downstream, upside down, followed by my two good paddles, and had rescued all three. Then they realized they might also have to search for two bodies. At this point, naturally, they called the local television station so that no good deed would go unrecorded.

We were grateful to be reunited with most of our stuff, and we thanked the Rescue Squad profusely. But when NBC5, the television news crew, sought an interview, we both said no. (This remains, I think, the only time I ever declined television coverage!) Nevertheless, they filmed us from afar. After putting my canoe on the car and retrieving our bicycles still at our put-in point, we drove home. We arrived in time to see our story lead the evening news, since we put human faces on the biggest weather story in Vermont that day, the continuing flood.

I hold that any canoe trip is a success if you can walk away from it. But maybe not, if you wind up featured on local TV.

I Lose My Paddle!

In 1995, after twenty years, I left Vermont and moved to our nation's capital. One reason I chose the District of Columbia was for the canoeing. Few outsiders realize it, but the Washington area offers everything from flat water and Class I rapids to terrifying Class VI, runnable only by world-class kayakers. And unlike Vermont, where most rivers are either too cold to paddle (in early spring) or too shallow (the rest of the year), rivers like the Potomac have enough water to be exciting all summer long.

One of the nicest runs is the "Shenandoah Staircase," the beautiful lower Shenandoah River just above its confluence with the Potomac at Harpers Ferry, 65 miles northwest of Washington, DC. The paddling club in the DC area, the Canoe Cruisers Association, paddles it often. My new DC girlfriend, Susan, agreed to go with me and join their trip. Harpers Ferry is a fascinating and beautiful small town well worth visiting even without canoeing as a draw. I had paddled the Staircase at least twice before, without incident. It was a beautiful warm Saturday in July. We would be with experienced river runners. What could possibly go wrong?

Because I still owned a convertible, we put the canoe on Susan's car and drove to the meeting point, which was also the take-out point. It was a gas station near Harpers Ferry and had a large parking lot where we could leave several cars.

At the gas station we met maybe twenty other paddlers and waited while they completed last-minute purchases at the attached convenience store. Unfortunately, Susan and I were new to each other, so we fell into a deep conversation, the way people do who are falling in love and are not yet used to it. After a few minutes, we looked up and were stunned to see that no car with a canoe or kayak on it remained in the parking lot. They had all driven off to the put-in point without us!

What to do?

Obviously we didn't want to drive all the way back to DC without paddling.

So we drove to a possible put-in point, left the car, and launched my canoe. I explained what to do if we upset. By now, you know the drill: hold on to your paddle, hold on to the canoe, stay upstream of the boat, and swim on your back with your feet downstream. We had on life jackets. It was a beautiful day, I knew the route, and I knew we could handle it. No, we weren't with the group anymore, but still, what could go wrong?

At first, nothing did. We started paddling back downstream toward our take-out point. We canoed down a series of Class II rapids, the kind I can take without too much difficulty. Susan was learning what to do when I called "Go right!" or "Go left!" I have always followed the rule of saying "Go" first, ever since I had a bow partner at Canoe Base who would yell just "Right!" Half of the time this meant, "Big rock on the right!" The rest of the time, he meant, "Go right!" The result was, exactly half the time we hit the rock. (You can do the math.) Saying "Go" eliminates the problem.

At first, we had a great time. As usual, choosing a path through the rapids put us into the present. I would stand up in the rear of the canoe as we reached each new set of riffles, trying to determine the best way through, since we didn't have the benefit of a group leader or other boats to watch. After we entered the rapids, Susan played a larger role, since she could see the hazards immediately in front of the bow better than I could in the stern. She remembered to say "Go" first, and we maneuvered from downstream V to downstream V without mishap. When we did hit a rock, it was only a glancing blow and the plastic canoe bounced off without sticking.

Late in the morning a couple of inflated rafts passed us by. Taking the Shenandoah Staircase in a six-person raft is absurd. It's like using a rope and pitons to climb, say, Bunker Hill. Rafting Class II rapids is mainly a pretext to lie back in the sun and drink beer, and sure enough, these college students were towing another little inflatable boat behind one raft, filled with a case of Bud Lite.

We stopped on a sand bar and ate the lunches we had brought. In the middle of the afternoon, however, Susan's body let her know that she had forgotten to take her prednisone, a cortisone drug. Susan has lupus, an autoimmune disease, and had to take fifteen milligrams each day to keep it under control. Not having any, her joints ached and she got serious pains in her ribs. Worse yet for our purposes, her hands swelled, making it hard to hold the paddle. We needed to end the trip as soon as we could and get back to her car, where she kept an emergency supply.

A little more paddling brought us to a place where we could hear traffic to our right from the highway above. We pulled over to the bank, got out, and proceeded to haul the canoe up a bank so steep it was almost a cliff. To this day, one of our family legend stories is about how impressed I was that Susan, this little 120-pound woman, hauled at least her half of our canoe up that hill on what amounted to perhaps our second "date."

Reaching the top, I stood by the highway and held out my paddle, an age-old signal separating me as a paddler from other more ordinary hitchhikers. Sure enough, it worked! A good ol' boy and his friend stopped in their pickup truck. He was driving right up the road to our put-in point, where

Susan's car was parked. I stashed my paddle in his pickup bed and climbed into the cab. A few minutes later, I arrived at her car.

Only as he drove away did I remember my paddle, still in his truck. I yelled and ran after the truck, but he didn't hear me.

Quickly I jotted down his license number. It was a beautiful wooden paddle, efficient and also a work of art, but I could retrieve it later.

I always hide my car keys in the woods near my car. Never do I take them down the river with me. I think this is good practice. Why? Well, first, they cannot unlock anything on the river, so why would I want them on it? Second, bad things might happen on the way down the river. For example, if the Lamoille River in flood can rip contact lenses out of my girlfriend's eyes, certainly it might find a way to get my car keys out of my swimsuit pocket. So now I retrieved my keys, or rather Susan's keys, from a nearby shrub, started her car, and drove back to retrieve Susan and my canoe.

Immediately she took her prednisone. Soon she started to feel OK again.

We put the canoe on top of the car, packed our remaining paddle, spare paddle, and other gear in the car, and got in. We didn't have time to do Harpers Ferry right, so we drove back home to DC. A successful trip, except I still had to recover my beautiful wooden paddle.

During the next week, I phoned the Maryland Department of Motor Vehicles and got the name, address, and phone number of my benefactor. I phoned him, thanked him again for the lift, and made a date to get my paddle the next Saturday evening.

When that day arrived, I drove off to his house. It turned out to be a mobile home in a wooded area in very rural Maryland, maybe 30 miles west of DC. When I got there, I found my friend impaired. I tried to find a paddling term to describe his problem, but the closest I could find was "three sheets to the wind." At least it's a nautical expression.[1]

In a confusing conversation, he seemed to tell me that he had left my paddle at his sister's house. It was now our task to drive over there to get it. First, however, he wanted to stop at his friend's house, just off the same road in the woods that we were on. His friend gave him another drink—a plastic cup with about six ounces of cold vodka. He offered me the same, but I was driving and thought better of it.

Then my friend told me confusedly how to get to his sister's house, where my paddle allegedly was. We drove back to the main road, turned west, and drove awhile, but somehow he never could tell me quite where to turn to find his sister's house. The additional vodka was taking its toll.

After almost an hour of this, I realized I wasn't likely to retrieve my paddle. Now my prime goal became to relieve myself of responsibility for my semicoherent charge.

We came upon a Holiday Inn, which offered at least a place where my friend might pee. He gave me the number of another relative of his, whom I called, while he then fell into a heavy slumber in an easy chair in the lobby. I thought his relative could come to the Inn and pick him up. They were not surprised by the call, and I inferred this was not the first time my friend had been incapacitated and they had been involved, but they made clear that they wanted no part of any such responsibility. I was on my own.

Briefly I considered just leaving him and driving away. After a while, the Holiday Inn would realize they had a problem, but it wouldn't be *my* problem; I would be safely home in bed in Washington, DC. But I wouldn't want to live with myself after so doing. After all, he had done me a favor the week before. I could not repay that favor by abandoning him.

So I woke him enough that he was able to walk to my car and get in before falling back asleep. Then I drove back toward his house. As we drove through the wooded road to his home, he woke up and grew more alert. He noticed a blue light flashing through the trees: a state police trooper was parked at his house, undoubtedly looking for him. So he had me stop the car a hundred yards away and he got out, planning to lie low in the woods until after they left.

I understood by then that he had my paddle, and I was not likely to get it back. But I also realized that his problems were far bigger than mine. So I wished him the best and never contacted him again.

And yes, now that I am without a paddle, maybe this is the proper time to call a halt to these little memoirs of my life with a paddle. This last trip had been outstanding. Susan and I had lived in the present. The weather had been warm and sunny. The valley had been beautiful. Our teamwork had been gratifying to experience. Indeed, we wound up married . . . to this day!

In fact, *all* my trips have been rewarding. Canoeing has added a precious icing to the cake of my life, helping me appreciate our beautiful planet while providing little anecdotes that have been, I hope, at least enjoyable, if not profound. Thank you for letting me share them with you.

Notes

1   Moreover, Gary Martin, who runs the website The Phrase Finder, cites "colleagues at CANOE, the *Committee to Ascribe a Nautical Origin to Everything*," for his extensive notes on the background of this phrase. (See Gary Martin, "The Meaning and Origin of the Expression: Three Sheets to the Wind," The Phrase Finder, https://www.phrases.org.uk/meanings/three-sheets-to-the-wind. html.) On water, a sheet is neither bed linen nor a sail but a rope, attached to the bottom part of a sail. Leaving three sheets "to the wind" meant the sail would flap uncontrollably and "the boat will lurch about like a drunken sailor," in Martin's words. My friend indeed lurched.

Reflections on Canoeing past Harpers Ferry

Most people know Harpers Ferry for its historical significance, of course, not its beautiful canoeing. George Washington established an armory and arsenal there in 1796; the town changed hands eight times during the Civil War, and Storer College, an important black institution, formed there in 1865 and dissolved in 1955. But three days in October 1859 put Harpers Ferry forever on the map of US history.

In my study as I type this is a framed copy of a print made from a photo of John Brown taken in about 1857, before he grew the beard that some now seem to think he always had. The picture, reproduced overleaf left, looks like a middle-aged businessman. That's because Brown was a middle-aged businessman. (Being an antislavery zealot didn't usually put food on the table.)

During my talks around the United States, I have shown this image to perhaps several thousand audience members, from middle school students to retirees. I ask them to put up their hands (silently!) if they recognize who I am showing. Two or three hands go up in an audience of hundreds. Then I show a much more familiar John Brown—gaunt, dramatically bearded, arms outstretched, sometimes holding a Bible and a gun, reproduced overleaf right. Most hands rise. This Brown looks disturbed, intense, even deranged; indeed, a tornado looms behind him. He also looks familiar. The image, painted by John Steuart Curry in

1937, is on display in the Kansas State Capitol. This, to most of my audience, is the *real* John Brown.

For most of the twentieth century, John Brown was considered crazy, as several textbooks still assure us. For some years, discussing whether he was crazed dominated a large part of the narrative presented by the National Park Service at Harpers Ferry, where he acted against slavery in 1859. I write about these matters in *Lies My Teacher Told Me*, so I won't repeat myself here, but every time I pass Harpers Ferry—on the river, in my car, or, most recently, on Amtrak's Capitol Limited train—I reflect again on Americans' tendency to use insanity as an explanation for social happenings: Hitler was insane. Maybe Stalin too. Certainly John Wilkes Booth was a madman; that's "why" he assassinated Abraham Lincoln.

Actually, insanity never explains any social event. Nor does the insanity "defense" explain criminal wrongdoing. It's not even supposed to. To plead insanity is to claim that "the accused was laboring under such a defect of reason, from disease of the mind, as not to know the nature and quality of the act he was doing or, if he did know it, that he did not know what he was doing was wrong."[1] Booth, Stalin, Hitler, Brown—all certainly knew what they were doing and knew that by most legal definitions of the time, their actions were deemed wrong.[2] Certainly all four of these actors told us why they did what they did, and none said he acted because he was crazy.

Moreover, none of these four acted alone. All had followers—in the cases of Hitler and Stalin, millions of followers. Similarly, Shelley Shannon did not act alone in 1993 when she shot abortion doctor George Tiller in both arms while he sat in his car. Indeed, another antiabortionist shot and killed Tiller in 2009, for the same reason.

So what do we do with all their followers and enablers? What do we make of the roughly two dozen men who accompanied John Brown? The women who helped at the Kennedy Farm before the raid? Were they all crazy too? Even the African Americans? What do we make of the masses of Germans who followed Hitler voluntarily, including those who did so before he took power? Surely considering the state of their mental health is inappropriate when trying to determine which social classes, age groups, gender, and so on tended to support the Nazis in 1932.[3]

Reactions to some recent mass murderers show Americans grappling more thoughtfully with the practice of labeling historical actors "insane." After Dylann Roof killed nine African Americans at church in Charleston, SC, in 2015, journalists used his belief in white supremacy, symbolized by his reverence for Confederate monuments, to help explain his actions. The main group arguing that he must have been insane were white nationalists, such as Andrew Anglin, editor of the Daily Stormer, a neo-Nazi website. They had an obvious reason to call him crazy, since otherwise they would be ideologically complicit in his crimes. In 2019, Nikki Haley, who as governor in 2015 had led South Carolina to stop flying the Confederate battle flag in a place of honor in front of its capitol, found herself arguing that the neo-Confederate use of the flag was "noble," reflecting "heritage and ancestry." Roof, on the hand, was not like that: "I will never understand the dark hatred that fills those people's hearts." Again, such a statement plays a useful role for Haley, separating her from the murderer,[4] but it avoids any effort to comprehend why Roof acted as he did. Our quest for understanding needs to be sociological, not psychological. The extreme members of a social movement—like Roof, Shannon, Booth, and yes, Brown—depend for logistical and ideological subsistence upon less extreme members. Thus those who support the continued public honoring of the Confederate flag and monuments do play a role in enabling people like Roof.

It was good that most journalists avoided calling Roof mad, because the label typically reveals more about the person doing the labeling than the person labeled. Consider the small band of Germans who tried to assassinate Adolf Hitler on July 20, 1944. Reading about their unrealistic goals, the worsening of their situation as the months of planning went on, and then their attempted coup even after it was clear that Hitler had survived, a historian could call them madmen. But no one has. Instead, it is the leader of the Third Reich, who took office partly because he promised to eliminate Jewish influence in Germany and then took steps to do just that, whose name gets more than a million Google hits when paired with "insane." Conversely, leaders of the Confederacy, who started a war to maintain and expand racial slavery, are never considered insane.[5] Rather, they are honored in stone in Southern state capitols, Washington, DC, and even Charleston, West Virginia, which seceded to avoid siding with the Confederacy in 1861. No statues of leaders of the Third Reich stand in Germany today. Surely that's because neo-Confederates won the Civil War in 1890, while Germany lost World War II.[6] As well, Germany has become antiracist, while the United States has not . . . although we have begun to move in that direction.

Most genetic explanations for social events are just as useless as "insanity" or "in their nature." Consider the claims, all too common in black America, that whites are racist "by nature" or that they perpetrated slavery and lynchings "because they are cruel." Racism is a product of history, not nature. "Cruelty" is not an explanation for inhumane behavior, merely a description of it.

I cannot expand this little reflection into a full-blown theory of racism.[7] Nor am I arguing that we should evaluate the sanity of Hitler's would-be killers or of Hitler himself. Quite the opposite: labeling Hitler insane merely puts him outside the realm of normal or acceptable behavior. It assures us that we are not like that, we would never do that. No normal person would. Hence we need not examine our own behavior or our own society to see in what ways, if any, we *are* like that.

Likewise, calling Booth a "madman" excuses us from having to think about white racism as a part of our social structure and a motivating force in our populace. As a result, most of us do not even learn in school that white supremacy was the key reason why he murdered Lincoln, as I have argued already in "Further Reflections on Lincoln in History."

John Brown remains controversial. As of the beginning of 2020, the National Park Service home page for Harpers Ferry did not even mention his name, though it had a whole page about Peregrine falcons found there. Few tourists and no history buffs visit Harpers Ferry to see the falcons, however. Avoiding the controversy doesn't make it go away and certainly doesn't help us become more thoughtful about Brown or slavery.

The next time you go anywhere near Harpers Ferry, take a day to enjoy your surroundings. "This is a beautiful country," John Brown said, as the wagon took him to his place of execution. Canoe the Shenandoah Staircase, or the Potomac above or below the Ferry. I've paddled all three. Do it with the Canoe Cruisers, though, not all by yourself. It's lovely. You'll live in the present.

But then take another day to live in the past. See what the National Park Service tells you and what they do not tell you about John Brown and slavery. In recent years NPS has taken seriously the call from Congress to treat slavery as the principal cause of secession and the Civil War, from Gettysburg to Corinth, Mississippi, and beyond. Sometimes at Harpers Ferry they do a great job, making Brown come alive in his philosophical and sociological complexity. Some rangers tell how Brown realized he might move American thinking about slavery even if he failed at Harpers Ferry—as indeed he did.

What the Park Service says about Brown, in turn, depends in part upon the position of Brown in our culture. In 2008, I attended the world premiere of Kirke Mechem's opera *John Brown*, in Kansas City. I bought a front-row seat and at intermission turned to the woman sitting next to me and asked her what she thought of it so far. She replied, "You know, if you had asked me ten years ago, I would have thought it was outlandish, because everybody "knew" John Brown was a madman. But then my friend here (and she gestured to the woman sitting to her right) introduced me to this book, *Lies My Teacher Told Me*, and it had quite a different perspective on John Brown. So I think the opera is pretty good." So had others: at the very first performance, a week earlier, "the crowd leapt to its feet and clapped so long and hard that hands grew sore," according to one reviewer.[8] Her friend turned out to have just retired from being superintendent of a nearby school district where, she said, she required all history and social studies teachers to read my book. Imagine the happy conversation that ensued when I confessed that I wrote it! I tell you that story not to brag, however, but to point out that you—*you*—also make a difference as to whether Americans find John Brown crazy or sane, or whether that's even a meaningful question, just as this school superintendent had done with her friend and her teachers. In turn, our view of Brown depends in part on the current state of race relations in America. Every time you bring up—at your workplace, choral group, canoe club, wherever—"Why are we so white?" you help others realize that one doesn't have to be crazy to care about ending racial separation.[9]

Invited by NPS, I have spoken twice at Harpers Ferry to park staff, but I am unlikely to do so again. Keeping all of them on point—by which I mean both forthright and accurate—will fall on *you*. The questions visitors ask, the issues they raise, can be an important source of improvement in the stories that historic sites tell. So, paddle hard, even on vacation!

Notes

1   This quote comes from the "M'Naghten rule," from 1843 England, the origin of today's insanity defense.

2   Stalin might have claimed that the cloak of state sanction made his actions legal. Certainly his courts made sure to follow legal forms, allowing defendants to confess, etc., even if the forms were shams and the confessions coerced.

3   Such an analysis is provided in William Sheridan Allen, *The Nazi Seizure of Power; The Experience of a Single German Town 1930–1935* (Chicago: Quadrangle, 1965).

4   Her "analysis" also helped her mend fences with neo-Confederates, who are overwhelmingly Republican, in case she wants to run for public office again. "Nikki Haley: My Position on the Confederate Flag Has Been Constant. Our Country's Culture Has Changed," *Washington Post*, December 11, 2019, http://washingtonpost. com/opinions/nikki-haley-todays-climate-wouldnt-allow-us-to-remove-the-confederate-flag-in-south-carolina/2019/12/11/ 67373682-1c3c-11ea-8d58-5ac3600967a1_story.html.

5   "Jefferson Davis" and "insane" do get lots of hits, but almost all of them turn out to refer to *other* people's alleged insanity—Brown's, Lincoln's, and the entire Union cause's!

6   I do know of Lee's surrender at Appomattox, not so far from Harpers Ferry. In *Lies My Teacher Told Me* and the early pages of *The Confederate and Neo-Confederate Reader* (Jackson: University Press of Mississippi, 2010), 15–20, I tell why I say the neo-Confederates won, ca. 1890.

7   Such a theory would require the term "cognitive dissonance," among other ideas, and would show that racism is a product of history, not biology, psychology, or genetics.

8   Alan Scherstuhl, "The Lyric Opera's World Premiere Is as Complicated as the Mythic Man Himself," *The Pitch*, May 8, 2008, https://www.thepitchkc.com/the-lyric-operas-world-premiere-is-as-complicated-as-the-mythical-man-himself/.

9   I admit that this paragraph reads as if aimed at nonblack readers. Few would accuse African Americans of mental illness or even "mere" fanaticism if they pushed for better race relations. Again, the way we tell our past minimizes white antiracism, including dispatching Brown as crazy, hence not a real example.

Paddling Hard

Having taken the last of my literal paddles, I now desire to contemplate once more the relationship between canoeing and life. My first conclusion derives from the series of misadventures this little memoir has recounted. To paraphrase Blanche in Tennessee Williams's *A Streetcar Named Desire*, my canoe trips have often depended on the kindness of strangers. Certainly any sense of excellence, derring-do, or even mere competence has been hard to maintain, given the number of times I have had to rely on help from passersby.

But I have concluded that my misadventures themselves have been a good thing. People *like* to help other people.

Until I got divorced, I thought it was somehow good, surely manly, to figure things out for oneself, bear burdens without complaint, and succeed owing to one's own efforts. Divorce and separation from my young children were too heavy a burden and too inexplicable for that, so I had no alternative but to talk with others, share the load, and ask for their insight and support.

To my surprise, doing so not only lightened my mood and woes but also strengthened my bonds with friends and relatives. They appreciated the trust my sharing represented, and mostly they responded wonderfully.

In this regard, river trips again imitate life. My canoe outings, even when they did *not* involve misadventures—and

yes, I did have "normal" trips too—usually involved help from others. Here I salute the fine men and women who organize trips with the Northern Vermont Canoe Cruisers in Burlington, the Canoe Cruisers in the DC metropolitan area, and the Potomac and Shenandoah Riverkeepers.[1] We who take your trips don't always thank you sufficiently. But you too benefit, I now understand, from the cooperative journeys that you organize, which, when you think about it, is exactly what life itself is.

Life has been short, but not *too* short. And I have paddled hard.[2]

Let me explain to you the particular river I chose to paddle and the particular incident that then influenced the specific channel I took.

As usual with human lives, chance played a role. In my social class, the firstborn son of a physician and a librarian, I was expected to go to college right after graduating from high school. The only real question was which college.

I applied to only two, Oberlin and Carleton, both

cerebral liberal arts colleges in the Midwest. I leaned toward Oberlin, partly because at that time it had the higher reputation. I had not visited either. In those days, before inexpensive air travel, out-of-state college visits were rare.

Then the all-male singing group the Knights of Carleton came to Decatur and gave a concert at an alum's house just a block down the street from my house. Carleton had notified me, and my parents and I went. I thought they sang all right, but more important, they were hilarious. These were my kind of people!

It was of course my first exposure to college humor. I'm sure if an Oberlin group had visited Decatur instead, I would have gone to Oberlin, but I wound up at Carleton College, in a small town in Minnesota, in the fall of 1960.

In turn, the winter of 1961–62, my sophomore year, was severe. Minnesota had three feet of snow on the ground for three months. It was not merely below freezing but below zero, day after day. By then I was becoming a sociologist, and sociology teaches us that human migrations typically require both a push and a pull.[3] In my case, the harsh winter of 1962 supplied the push, prompting me to look for somewhere else to spend the winter of 1963. At the same time, friends of mine majoring in French were spending their junior year abroad in France. Friends in political science were enrolling in the Washington Semester at American University. How might I become a competent sociologist, never having lived outside the Midwest? I did not consider that competent. I decided to spend part of my junior year "abroad," in Mississippi.

I arranged to spend Carleton's winter term, January through March, at Mississippi State University. It was then the largest "all-white" university in the world outside of South Africa, as some students told me with pride, others with chagrin. (I put "all-white" in quotation marks because Chinese American students from the Mississippi Delta also attended, having graduated from "white" public high schools.)

Soon after I arrived at Mississippi State, I learned of the existence of Tougaloo College and Ernst Borinski, its famous professor of sociology. After he died in 1983, a book (*From Swastika to Jim Crow*), movie, and museum exhibit came out about him, along with three or four other Jewish professors who had likewise escaped Germany and wound up at black colleges.[4] Sociologists at Mississippi State insisted that I should meet him, and of course my purpose in spending time in the South was to experience different cultures, not just Mississippi State, so I immediately wrote Borinski. I asked if I could spend a few days as a student at Tougaloo.

I enjoyed my months at Mississippi State and learned a lot, but it was very different from Carleton. One difference related to books, or, rather, their absence. Generally, students at Mississippi State didn't read books. As a (budding) sociologist, I knew I needed data to prove that impression, so I counted all the books owned by all the students in my dormitory wing. There were twelve double rooms housing 23 students. (I did not include myself.) I counted every book they had in their rooms—pulp novels, even comic books— but not textbooks. I was interested only in books bought voluntarily.

The 23 students owned 51 books. One owned 42. He was an intellectual. Another owned maybe five. A couple of others owned one or two.

That was it. Most of my dorm-mates had no books in their rooms and may have never owned one, other than those required for class. The mode, the best average to use for this distribution, was zero. So was the median. The contrast to Carleton, an intellectual monastery, was stunning. Many Carleton students owned 51 books all by themselves.

Tougaloo was different. It had a thriving intellectual subculture. After I got there, I counted all the books owned by my four roommates, again excluding textbooks. (One roommate was away on exchange at Oberlin, which is why his bed was available to me, but his stuff was still there, so I could count his books.) The four owned 48 books among them, about a dozen each. A mode of twelve is infinitely more than a mode of zero, both in multiplication and culture. Consequently Tougaloo made quite an impression on me. So did its overt support for the Civil Rights Movement, from the president on down.[5]

Two years later, I got Dr. Borinski to hire me to work for the summer at his Social Science Lab and run the Social Science Forum, the only place in central Mississippi where ideas could be discussed across racial lines. Then, in 1968, when I finished my PhD in sociology at Harvard, Tougaloo hired me to teach sociology.

There, at the beginning of my second semester of full-time teaching, I had an "aha moment," or perhaps it should be called an "oh no moment."[6] My first-year students at Tougaloo knew a completely distorted white-supremacist view of Mississippi's past, particularly of its important Reconstruction history.

This was no accident. As part of its response to *Brown*, the 1954 school desegregation decision, Mississippi's all-white legislature passed a law requiring that state history be taught twice, in fifth and ninth grades. Both courses were to be taught in a way that maintained "our Southern way of life." I realized that the lawmakers knew exactly what they were doing. If black Mississippians were convinced, as my first-year students were at Tougaloo in 1969, that during Reconstruction, the one time they had been center stage in Mississippi history, they had "screwed up," that undercut their certainty that they should be electing public officials today. Even worse, young white Mississippians learned that they had better keep African Americans disfranchised, because "look what happened last time."

Eventually I responded to this terrible situation by getting a grant and recruiting students and professors from Tougaloo and from Millsaps, the nearby white college, to write a new textbook, *Mississippi: Conflict and Change*, for the ninth-grade course. Then, even though Mississippi usually adopted three to five books per subject area, and even though only two had been submitted in Mississippi history, the state textbook board rejected our book. The vote was two to five, and on the rating committee were two African Americans and five Caucasians. You can do the math.

Eventually this rejection led to the lawsuit *Loewen et al. v. Turnipseed et al.*, filed in the Northern District of Mississippi US District Court, which resulted in a stunning victory in 1980. Now our book was on the approved list, yet less than a fifth of Mississippi's more than 150 school districts adopted it.

Years later, we were vindicated. The cover article of the *Journal of Mississippi History* for Spring 2010, "The Evolution of Race in Mississippi History Textbooks, 1900–1995," examined about eighteen textbooks. Historian Rebecca M. Davis pointed out that the usual portrayal of Mississippi's past in these books "created a fundamental misunderstanding." She specifically emphasized the textbook we were opposing as an example of this genre, "woefully behind the times" and based on "outdated research." Repeatedly she emphasized that "*Conflict and Change* displayed a dramatic shift in textbook representations of race and racism," freeing later authors to be more honest than they otherwise would have been. Seven years later, Charles Eagles, a historian ironically located at the University of Mississippi, wrote an entire book about our book and lawsuit.[7] Although we had not reached the teeming masses of high school students as we had hoped to, we had transformed the materials available for Mississippians to learn about their past.[8]

In 1974 the president of Tougaloo took a step I could not stomach. On his own, he signed the college up for ROTC, the Reserve Officer Training Corps of the US Army. The Vietnam War was still going on, although most US troops had been withdrawn. ROTC prepared college students to become officers in the army. Student protests of the war had driven ROTC from many northern campuses. The army responded in part by opening new programs at black colleges. Many students and professors at Tougaloo felt that ROTC was particularly inappropriate for our beloved institution, since it had played such a critiquing role in Mississippi and the United States on behalf of social justice. Students voted two to one against the move, and all thirteen members of the veterans' club came out against it. The faculty would have voted it down, but the president packed the faculty meeting with administrators who were said to have faculty co-appointments and who voted approval.

Someone had to make a statement, so early in 1975 I resigned, leaving behind a statement telling why. Besides, the canoeing was terrible: Mississippi's rivers flow a bit more than the Sangamon, but they are the same brown color and offer no whitewater challenges.

Near the end of 1975 I left Mississippi and took up teaching duties at the University of Vermont. I still joke that I taught at "the blackest and the whitest institutions of higher education in America." Paradoxically, "UVM" already had ROTC, but at least the paddling was better. And somehow UVM was always "they," while Tougaloo had been "we," so I did not feel so personally implicated in its sins.

At UVM, my exposure to what American high schools teach about the past continued, thanks to hordes of first-year students in huge classes in "introductory sociology," almost 60% of whom came from out of state. Soon I realized that misunderstanding US history—believing all kinds of stories that never happened, coupled with ignorance of many other events that *did* take place and were of profound importance—was hardly confined to the Deep South. Mississippi merely exemplified in a more exaggerated form a problem pervasive throughout the United States, as it exemplified other problems in more exaggerated form.

I also realized that if Mississippi's white power structure was absolutely right in concluding that miseducating K–12 students could help maintain white supremacy, then educating them accurately could help bring about social justice, on racial and other lines. Eventually, this realization led to my email signature: "Telling the truth about the past helps cause justice in the present. Achieving justice in the present helps us tell the truth about the past." Earlier, beginning in the 1980s, it led to my writing the best seller *Lies My Teacher Told Me*, about what we get wrong about US history nationally.

Some of you are reading this little memoir because you found *Lies My Teacher Told Me* valuable. Maybe if I tell you something of the response I have received over the years from folks who read and were influenced by that book, this chapter will give you a framework to understand its importance. Conversely, maybe the chapter will give those of you who have never read anything else I've written some reason to try another book of mine.

Over the years since 1995, when *Lies My Teacher Told Me* first came out, its success was always due to reader reaction. Beginning on the West Coast, libraries "can't keep it on their shelves" owing to public demand, according to a Bay Area publication. Briefly *Lies* became a best seller, first in San Francisco, then Seattle, and later Boston and Los Angeles. In 2019, as I write this, the new printing of *Lies* was the best-selling book at Powell's, in Portland, Oregon, said to be the largest bookstore in the world. Almost from the first day it came out, *Lies* has been the best-selling book in its category, historiography, at that other large bookstore, Amazon.

Readers did this. My publisher, The New Press, was indeed new, even fledgling, and had neither the resources nor the knowledge to kindle such a response.[9] One reader told me he had put copies in 25 black barber shops in the St. Louis metropolitan area, hoping to cure the same false racial consciousness that my Tougaloo students had displayed. Other readers repeatedly joined the Quality Paperback Book Club, which featured *Lies* for several years. For their four free books, they would choose four copies of *Lies*. Then later they would buy one more, thus fulfilling their membership obligation, quit, and repeat the process.

Over the years and continuing today, I have gotten the most extraordinary emails. At least once a month someone writes me, "Your book changed my life." Three different investment bankers or mergers and acquisitions lawyers wrote me to say that after reading *Lies* they gave up those jobs, with their high six-figure incomes, to become high school history and social studies teachers. Other readers at the opposite end of our socioeconomic hierarchy—college dropouts, warehouse workers, even homeless folks—were inspired to get a GED and return to college to become teachers so they could pass on this new information and get students thinking. "I went from the kid who was having truancy problems to taking Advanced Placement US History," reported a high school student in Minneapolis.[10]

Most fun was an email I got way back in 1996, shortly after the paperback came out: "I really like your book, *Lies My Teacher Told Me*. I've been using it to heckle my history teacher from the back of the room. My friends all like the book too, and if I could get a group price on it from the publisher, I could sell it in the corridors of my high school."

Of course, I forwarded his email immediately to the publisher and a day or so later received a reply with a good discount. I sent it on to the student, only to hear back from him for the second and last time: "Thank you very much for the group price on *Lies My Teacher Told Me*. However, I have to put my plan to sell your book in high school on hold, because tomorrow I'm getting expelled for failing to stand up for the pledge of allegiance."

The book has special appeal to Native Americans, African Americans, and homeschoolers. "Your description of the Indian experience in the United States and, more importantly, the concept of a syncretic American society has subtly, but powerfully, changed my understanding of my country, and, in fact, my own ancestry," wrote a Native American from New England.

A professor in Virginia wrote me, "My students, who are all African Americans, were immensely enthused and energized by your book." One of his students chimed in: "In this one book, I have learned more than I did in my four years of high school history." Homeschoolers are a bifurcated population; those who are not fundamentalist Protestants often use *Lies* as a basic text, along with *Lies Across America*, which they use to help their kids critique historic sites when they visit them.

Most readers realized that the book bashed neither teachers nor our country. "Your book has given me a new outlook, yet a strong appreciation for our country," as one eighth grade history teacher put it. Even first grade teachers have grown "appalled at what I was teaching my class about Columbus and Thanksgiving which I believed to be true," as one wrote.

In a sense, *Lies My Teacher Told Me*, like *Mississippi: Conflict and Change*, failed. Certainly it did not prompt publishers to revise their textbooks. But it did trigger considerable change in how schools of education prepare students to teach history and social studies. As well, many school districts now require their teachers in this area to read *Lies* or the book I aimed specifically at teachers, *Teaching What Really Happened*.

I tried to make a difference in person, as well, and have now given more than 500 talks and workshops at colleges, school districts, Indian reservations, and other institutions, hoping to get teachers to teach "against" their textbooks rather than simply having students memorize them.

I also tried to get well-known historians engaged by textbook publishers as "authors" to actually write "their" textbooks. After all, I argued, when will they get another opportunity to reach a million or more young minds, across the nation. But they knew that the history profession does not read or review high school history textbooks, so they just took the money and never bothered to write or even read the history that went out with their names attached.[11] They did not paddle hard.

K–12 history is important, because studies show that only one American in six ever takes a course in history after high school. Where then do we learn about our past as adults? I came to realize the important of public history: museums, plantations, historic homes, historical markers, and monuments. Unfortunately, our public history suffers from the same distortions, omissions, even lies, that plague our textbooks. My next book, *Lies Across America*, exposed these problems. It became the best-selling work in public history. Perhaps it made more of a difference than *Lies My Teacher Told Me*, because it led directly to new markers, changes in existing historic home presentations, and even the removal of some Confederate monuments, all described in the second edition of *Lies Across America*, which came out in 2019.

When you go paddling, you will notice that most of your fellow paddlers are white. Racism plays a role here. Many African Americans are wary of venturing into rural and small-town America, national parks, rivers, and lakes—unsure if they will be welcomed or harassed. Some Latinos feel the same. They are not being paranoid. My earlier "Reflection on Oral History" told how racial minorities got concentrated into urban areas between 1890 and 1940, when sundown towns—"all-white" on purpose—were forming across the North.

After finishing *Lies Across America* in 1999, I sought advice from colleagues in sociology and history about what I should write next. I offered three choices: a textbook for introductory sociology, a book treating unexpected places that get history right, or one about sundown towns. Although I didn't know it at the time, in retrospect I am so glad I chose sundown towns.

When I started working on sundown towns, nobody had any idea what I was getting myself into, least of all me. Having grown up in Illinois, I planned more research in that state than in any other single place, but it would be a national undertaking. I expected to find maybe 10 sundown towns in Illinois, 50 across the country. I now estimate that about 507 towns went sundown, formally or informally, in Illinois alone—two-thirds of all communities in the state! While I have proven that estimate in my book *Sundown Towns*, my similar estimates for other Northern states, such as Oregon, Indiana, and Pennsylvania, are more speculative. Inadvertently, I opened an entire new sphere of research! In a few areas—Arkansas, the suburbs of Los Angeles, perhaps Colorado—other researchers have stepped up and are filling this gap. Otherwise, I continue my own work on the subject, trying to confirm every sundown town in America at my website, but as the next chapter, "Canoeing Niagara," tells, I'm dying. I'll never finish.

Finally, I would not want to be pigeonholed politically. Some readers dismiss me as a "leftist." Careful reading of *Lies*, along with listening to my spoken lecture about capitalism included in my audiobook *Rethinking Our Past*, should prevent that.[12] As one former high school history teacher put it, "I never could decide whether you were a Socialist or a Republican." A few readers have accused me of inadequate patriotism, but more people agree with an English professor in Ohio who wrote, "Having just completed this important work, I feel so much more optimistic about the future of our country."

As a canoe paddler, I usually tried to stay in the middle of the stream, not favoring either bank a priori. I paddled on the left and on the right. I recommend you do the same. If you don't know folks who hold very different views from yours about, say, abortion, widen your circle of friends, or at least of acquaintances.

How do you go about meeting people unlike yourself? Well, one good way is on the river!

Notes

1 The Riverkeepers not only organize trips but also take legal and social actions to make rivers safe to canoe and to drink.
2 I do hope, so very much, that you agree.
3 The Great Migration of African Americans to Northern cities, for example, was triggered by the terrible human rights abuses across the South following 1890, coupled with the stories, often exaggerated, of occupational success by blacks in Detroit and other Northern cities. As Alice Walker noted in her early poem "Uncles," every Southern black family had relatives "up North," and "It was their *job* / to come home every summer / from the North . . . And make my mother / Cry and long / For Denver, Jersey City, Philadelphia . . ." Walker, "Uncles," in *Revolutionary Petunias* (New York: Harcourt, Brace, Jovanovich, 1973), 9.
4 The museum exhibit is titled *Beyond Swastika and Jim Crow*.
5 Most black colleges in the South wanted nothing to do with the civil rights movement. Spelman, for example, fired Prof. Howard Zinn because he would not give up his civil rights activities
6 I tell this story in *Teaching What Really Happened* (New York: Teachers College Press, 2018 [2009]), 2–7.
7 Rebecca M. Davis, "The Three R's—Reading, 'Riting, and Race: The Evolution of Race in Mississippi History Textbooks, 1900-1995," *Journal of Mississippi History* 72, no. 1 (Spring 2010): 10, 25; Charles W. Eagles, *Civil Rights, Culture Wars: The Fight over a Mississippi Textbook* (Chapel Hill: University of North Carolina Press, 2017).

8   I don't mean to be sanguine about our failure to win more adoptions. While I have not reviewed the textbooks in Mississippi history that followed ours, I suspect they are less forthright in their treatment of white supremacy and less oriented to getting students to think critically. So I lament the two generations of students who didn't get a chance to experience *Mississippi: Conflict and Change.*

9   Just for the record, in my experience other larger publishers know little about how to sell books too.

10 Today, December 10, 2019, for example, I put the finishing touches on this essay. This morning, I got an email from a college administrator at the University of Texas that said, "I know you've heard this to the point of cliché, but your book changed my whole trajectory in life."

11 See Loewen, "Farewell to the U.S. History Textbook?" History News Network (HNN), February 27, 2018, http:///hnn.us/blog/154069; Loewen, "On the Amazing Similarity between the New Texas Textbook Standards and the Textbook, *The Americans*: An Open Letter to Gerald A. Danzer," HNN, July 29, 2015, https://historynewsnetwork.org/blog/153654; and Diana Jean Schemo, "Schoolbooks Are Given F's in Originality," *New York Times*, July 13, 2006.

12 Loewen, *Rethinking Our Past* (Prince Frederick, MD: Recorded Books, 2005).

Canoeing Niagara

I no longer venture onto rivers. Now I near the end of that greatest river of all, my life journey. Facing near-certain death from stage IV muscle-invasive metastatic bladder cancer—it's the modifiers that do you in—I have learned one final way that, I hope, life can imitate a canoe trip: the Niagara simile. Everyone with terminal cancer, I have learned, wants it to be like Niagara. You see, upstream of Niagara Falls, the Niagara River hardly flows. It forms a lake. People swim and picnic. Paddling is easy. No problem. Then, as you approach the falls, with only the warning of a roaring in your ears, suddenly, all in a rush, you're over. No open canoeist could hope to survive that final drop.

I only hope to be so lucky.

Already I have lived to be 78. My imminent death cannot be construed as a tragedy. My children are well grown. Theirs are coming along. My life's work is, I submit, done.

Since I never retired, I still must convince myself that, as Walt Whitman put it, "To take interest is well, and not to take interest shall be well." Concerning canoeing, I have reached that point. About life, and society, not so much. Thus far, I am instead reminded of a Vermont joke. Vermont, you may know, is a state that has jokes. Most states do not. Some states are known to be the butt of others' jokes, such as the cruel and misleading anecdotes told about West Virginians in neighboring states. But Vermonters tell their own jokes— wry, a bit sly, often showing some wisdom. This one is not as funny as some, but it fits my current circumstances.

You need to know that Vermont is also one of those states where it matters a great deal whether you are or are not "native." In Illinois, some say "Illinoisan," some say "Illinoisian," no one knows whether to pronounce the "s" or not, and no one cares anyway. Massachusetts does not even have a name for it—"Massachusettsian"? But to be a native Vermonter is an important part of one's identity in the Green Mountain state. So a "flatland" tourist finds herself asking an aged Vermonter, at least in his 80s, "Have you lived in Vermont your whole life?"

Comes the laconic reply, "Not yet."

I have often been asked, "Have you really worked on social justice and accurate history your whole life?"

Still, my answer must be "Not yet."

But I shall get to yes.[1]

Meanwhile, those of you who still have, hopefully, many years before you need to get to yes: please consider dedicating *your* whole life to social justice, accurate history, or another issue of equal importance.[2] America is up several creeks just now that need our attention. And each of us does have a paddle.

Of course, such dedication need not be monochromatic. Indeed, a life without variety would probably drive most of us bonkers. I cannot claim that my canoe trips had anything to do with accurate history or decreasing racism. They enriched my life, were fun, and provided memories that, with a bit of luck, amused you. Still, the core of my life had purpose, and I hope the core of yours does too. You want "to work hard at work worth doing." Then, when you get to your Niagara, you will feel—even *know*—that you used such gifts as you possessed for, not against, the people.[3]

Notes

1   I must supply for you two poems and a song that I have given to friends facing death or mourning the loss of loved ones and that now are proving useful to me: the passage beginning "Come, Lovely and Soothing Death" from Walt Whitman's "When Lilacs Last in the Dooryard Bloom'd"; "Thanatopsis," by William Cullen Bryant; and the final song, "Der Abschied" or "The Farewell," from Gustav Mahler's *Das Lied von der Erde* ("The Song of the Earth"). Widely available on the web, may they prove stalwart companions to both of us when we need to call upon them!

2   What of our increasing human threat to the environment? What about the fact that our great nation has been at war almost every year since I was born? (That was 1942. *You* do the math!) What about sexism, which in complementary ways still limits the lives of both men and women? Or less obvious choices, such as our increasing Nature Deficit Disorder, or whatever causes *you* choose?

3   This last turn of phrase originated with the great American architect, Louis H. Sullivan, who wrote in *Kindergarten Chats and Other writings* (New York: George Wittenborn, 1947 [1918], 151: "In a democracy there can be but one test of citizenship, namely: Are you using such gifts, such powers as you possess, for or against the . . . people?"

Postscript: Paddling after Niagara

With supreme self-confidence, Walt Whitman in *Leaves of Grass* knew he was immortal. He ended "Song of Myself" with these enduring words:

> Missing me one place search another,
> I stop somewhere waiting for you.

I wish I had his self-assurance! Then I could write,

> Seek me in the easy Class II rapids.
> Remember me when you have your own paddling
>   fiascoes
> and must rely upon the kindness of strangers.

Instead, I am using what time remains to leave for your use some tools that you may find useful as you work, as I hope you will, to tell the truth about the past and achieve justice in the present. In this task, as on my canoe trips, I have relied once more upon the kindness of others—strangers at first, but now becoming boon companions.

I had always expected to die shortly after my 94th birthday, which would have been February 6, 2036, and I had planned fifteen more years of intense antiracist work for the interim—about sundown towns, still-extant Confederate monuments, and other intersections between lies we still tell about our past and injustices we still perpetuate in the present.[1]

This is not to be. Yet in the same weeks I have spent

finishing this little memoir, I have also been working to help the twin causes of accurate history and social justice live on after my demise. Recently I met with a young scholar, a tenured professor of history at the University of Michigan, who will take over much of my intellectual work, including my research on sundown towns, on public history, and against Confederate monuments. More recently I met with the President of Tougaloo College, the courageous black institution in Mississippi that houses my website; with a graduate of Tougaloo who is an attorney in DC; with the investment adviser who advises the funds I am leaving Tougaloo to continue the website; with idealistic antiracist computer people from California and Illinois who will maintain it; and with an antiracist activist from Kentucky, who will form a board of advisers for the site. They will continue on the web some of the activities that occupied most of my life during the past several decades.

Visitors to this website—sundown.tougaloo.edu—will find many projects that use accurate history to cause social justice in the present. For example, a three-page paper tells "How to Confirm Sundown Towns." Other stories tell how to use that information, once you have gathered it, to get a community to transcend its white supremacist past.

Another fun page lists the "Top Ten Silliest Historical Sites." You might find a similarly wrong marker, museum exhibit, or monument near you and propose its revision. If you do your homework well, the agency in charge will have a hard time denying you, especially if you bring on board historians, students, and leaders of various constituencies.

Yet another page offers you a quiz in US history. You'll probably flunk it but will have more fun than you did passing any multiple-choice history quiz you took in high school. Many other pages on my site will suggest ways to get students interested in doing history, not merely being bored by "learning" it. I hope it is a resource for teachers and everyone working toward accurate history and social justice.

Finally, there are ways for you to contribute, whether you have a suggestion for a really good historical site, a sundown town anecdote to relate, a way you used one of my books creatively, or some other idea. You will find portals throughout the website that will lead to the team that maintains it. In this way, the website will have a life of its own, after I do not. Remember Abraham Lincoln's words, after he lost to Stephen A. Douglas in 1858: "The cause of civil liberty must not be surrendered at the end of *one*, or even, one *hundred* defeats."[2] Neither must the interrelated causes of equality and truth today—or whatever cause is crucial to you.

Then, when asked in some future existence, if any, "Did you really work on social justice and accurate history your whole life?" I can reply, referencing you, "And then some!"

More important, *you* will be paddling hard, revealing truth, sparking justice, and enjoying the sparkling stream of life. And then, nothing can possibly go wrong.

Notes

1   I had also intended to write three volumes of memoirs: *Living on the Color Line*, about my years in Mississippi and Vermont; *Life at Gender Gap*, about my checkered relationships with women; and *At Home at the Range*, tales of my cooking adventures and misadventures. And I had planned a third volume in my "Lies" series, to be called something like *Lies Avoided: Unexpected Places That Get History Right*, because across our great nation, all kinds of historic sites, some unfortunately obscure, tell important parts of our past that most of us never learned, and do so well.

2   Abraham Lincoln, letter to Henry Asbury, November 19, 1858 (his italics).

About the Author

James W. Loewen is the author of *Lies My Teacher Told Me: Everything Your High School History Textbook Got Wrong*, the best-selling book by a living sociologist. He also wrote *Lies Across America: What Our Historic Sites Get Wrong*, which has played a major role in getting Americans to question our Confederate public history and helped historic sites treat difficult topics like sexual orientation. *Sundown Towns* helped Americans realize that all-white towns were common and intentional across the North and the West. Some have since publicly apologized. In 2012 the American Sociological Association gave Loewen its Cox/Johnson/Frazier Award, named for three African American sociological pioneers; he is the first white person to win this award.

Also by James W. Loewen
The Mississippi Chinese: Between Black and White
Mississippi: Conflict and Change (with co-authors)
Social Science in the Courtroom
Lies My Teacher Told Me about Christopher Columbus
Lies My Teacher Told Me
Lies Across America
Sundown Towns
Teaching What Really Happened
The Confederate and Neo-Confederate Reader (with co-editor)

ABOUT PM PRESS

PM Press is an independent, radical publisher of books and media to educate, entertain, and inspire. Founded in 2007 by a small group of people with decades of publishing, media, and organizing experience, PM Press amplifies the voices of radical authors, artists, and activists. Our aim is to deliver bold political ideas and vital stories to all walks of life and arm the dreamers to demand the impossible. We have sold millions of copies of our books, most often one at a time, face to face. We're old enough to know what we're doing and young enough to know what's at stake. Join us to create a better world.

PM Press
PO Box 23912
Oakland, CA 94623
www.pmpress.org

PM Press in Europe
europe@pmpress.org
www.pmpress.org.uk

FRIENDS OF PM PRESS

These are indisputably momentous times—the financial system is melting down globally and the Empire is stumbling. Now more than ever there is a vital need for radical ideas.

In the years since its founding—and on a mere shoestring—PM Press has risen to the formidable challenge of publishing and distributing knowledge and entertainment for the struggles ahead. With over 450 releases to date, we have published an impressive and stimulating array of literature, art, music, politics, and culture. Using every available medium, we've succeeded in connecting those hungry for ideas and information to those putting them into practice.

Friends of PM allows you to directly help impact, amplify, and revitalize the discourse and actions of radical writers, filmmakers, and artists. It provides us with a stable foundation from which we can build upon our early successes and provides a much-needed subsidy for the materials that can't necessarily pay their own way. You can help make that happen—and receive every new title automatically delivered to your door once a month—by joining as a Friend of PM Press. And, we'll throw in a free T-shirt when you sign up.

Here are your options:

- **$30 a month** Get all books and pamphlets plus 50% discount on all webstore purchases

- **$40 a month** Get all PM Press releases (including CDs and DVDs) plus 50% discount on all webstore purchases

- **$100 a month** Superstar—Everything plus PM merchandise, free downloads, and 50% discount on all webstore purchases

For those who can't afford $30 or more a month, we have **Sustainer Rates** at $15, $10 and $5. Sustainers get a free PM Press T-shirt and a 50% discount on all purchases from our website.

Your Visa or Mastercard will be billed once a month, until you tell us to stop. Or until our efforts succeed in bringing the revolution around. Or the financial meltdown of Capital makes plastic redundant. Whichever comes first.

Understanding Jim Crow: Using Racist Memorabilia to Teach Tolerance and Promote Social Justice

David Pilgrim with a foreword by Henry Louis Gates Jr.

ISBN: 978-1-62963-114-1
$24.95   208 pages

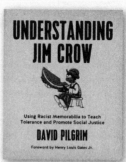

For many people, especially those who came of age after landmark civil rights legislation was passed, it is difficult to understand what it was like to be an African American living under Jim Crow segregation in the United States. Most young Americans have little or no knowledge about restrictive covenants, literacy tests, poll taxes, lynchings, and other oppressive features of the Jim Crow racial hierarchy. Even those who have some familiarity with the period may initially view racist segregation and injustices as mere relics of a distant, shameful past. A a proper understanding of race relations in this country must include a solid knowledge of Jim Crow—how it emerged, what it was like, how it ended, and its impact on the culture.

Understanding Jim Crow introduces readers to the Jim Crow Museum of Racist Memorabilia, a collection of more than ten thousand contemptible collectibles that are used to engage visitors in intense and intelligent discussions about race, race relations, and racism. The items are offensive. They were meant to be offensive. The items in the Jim Crow Museum served to dehumanize blacks and legitimized patterns of prejudice, discrimination, and segregation.

Using racist objects as teaching tools seems counterintuitive—and, quite frankly, needlessly risky. Many Americans are already apprehensive discussing race relations, especially in settings where their ideas are challenged. The museum and this book exist to help overcome our collective trepidation and reluctance to talk about race.

Fully illustrated, and with context provided by the museum's founder and director David Pilgrim, *Understanding Jim Crow* is both a grisly tour through America's past and an auspicious starting point for racial understanding and healing.

Teaching Resistance: Radicals, Revolutionaries, and Cultural Subversives in the Classroom

Edited by John Mink

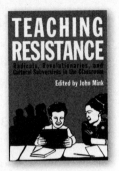

ISBN: 978-1-62963-709-9
$24.95   416 pages

Teaching Resistance is a collection of the voices of activist educators from around the world who engage inside and outside the classroom from pre-kindergarten to university and emphasize teaching radical practice from the field. Written in accessible language, this book is for anyone who wants to explore new ways to subvert educational systems and institutions, collectively transform educational spaces, and empower students and other teachers to fight for genuine change. Topics include community self-defense, Black Lives Matter and critical race theory, intersections between punk/DIY subculture and teaching, ESL, anarchist education, Palestinian resistance, trauma, working-class education, prison teaching, the resurgence of (and resistance to) the Far Right, special education, antifascist pedagogies, and more.

Edited by social studies teacher, author, and punk musician John Mink, the book features expanded entries from the monthly column in the politically insurgent punk magazine *Maximum Rocknroll*, plus new works and extensive interviews with subversive educators. Contributing teachers include Michelle Cruz Gonzales, Dwayne Dixon, Martín Sorrondeguy, Alice Bag, Miriam Klein Stahl, Ron Scapp, Kadijah Means, Mimi Nguyen, Murad Tamini, Yvette Felarca, Jessica Mills, and others, all of whom are unified against oppression and readily use their classrooms to fight for human liberation, social justice, systemic change, and true equality.

Royalties will be donated to Teachers 4 Social Justice: t4sj.org

"Teaching Resistance *brings us the voices of activist educators who are fighting back inside and outside of the classroom. The punk rock spirit of this collection of concise, hard-hitting essays is bound to stir up trouble.*"
—Mark Bray, historian, author of *Antifa: The Anti-Fascist Handbook* and coeditor of *Anarchist Education and the Modern School: A Francisco Ferrer Reader*

Strike! 50th Anniversary Edition

Jeremy Brecher with a Preface by Sara Nelson and a Foreword by Kim Kelly

ISBN: 978-1-62963-800-3
$28.95   640 pages

Jeremy Brecher's *Strike!* narrates the dramatic story of repeated, massive, and sometimes violent revolts by ordinary working people in America. Involving nationwide general strikes, the seizure of vast industrial establishments, nonviolent direct action on a massive scale, and armed battles with artillery and tanks, this exciting hidden history is told from the point of view of the rank-and-file workers who lived it. Encompassing the repeated repression of workers' rebellions by company-sponsored violence, local police, state militias, and the U.S. Army and National Guard, it reveals a dimension of American history rarely found in the usual high school or college history course.

Since its original publication in 1972, no book has done as much as *Strike!* to bring U.S. labor history to a wide audience. Now this fiftieth anniversary edition brings the story up to date with chapters covering the "mini-revolts of the twenty-first century," including Occupy Wall Street and the Fight for Fifteen. The new edition contains over a hundred pages of new materials and concludes by examining a wide range of current struggles, ranging from #BlackLivesMatter, to the great wave of teachers strikes "for the soul of public education," to the global "Student Strike for Climate," that may be harbingers of mass strikes to come.

"Jeremy Brecher's *Strike!* is a classic of American historical writing. This new edition, bringing his account up to the present, comes amid rampant inequality and growing popular resistance. No book could be more timely for those seeking the roots of our current condition."
—Eric Foner, Pulitzer Prize winner and DeWitt Clinton Professor of History at Columbia University

"Magnificent—a vivid, muscular labor history, just updated and rereleased by PM Press, which should be at the side of anyone who wants to understand the deep structure of force and counterforce in America."
—JoAnn Wypijewski, author of *Killing Trayvons: An Anthology of American Violence*